No-Compromise Retirement Plan

OVERCOMING THE COMPROMISES IN YOUR IRA
TO LIVE A MORE SECURE RETIREMENT

Martin H. Ruby
with Neil Wilding & Becky Swansburg

Stonewood Financial
LOUISVILLE, KENTUCKY

Copyright © 2019 by Martin H. Ruby.

All rights reserved. No part of this publication may be reproduced, distributed or transmitted in any form or by any means, including photocopying, recording, or other electronic or mechanical methods, without the prior written permission of the publisher, except in the case of brief quotations embodied in critical reviews and certain other noncommercial uses permitted by copyright law.

Martin H. Ruby/Stonewood Financial
950 Breckenridge Lane, Suite 130
Louisville, KY 40207
www.StonewoodFinancialSolutions.com

Book layout ©2013 BookDesignTemplates.com

The No-Compromise Retirement Plan/ Martin H. Ruby with Neil Wilding & Becky Swansburg. —2nd ed.
ISBN 9781799142980

Contents

Prologue i
    Help From an Actuary i
    Putting Actuarial Expertise on Your Side ii
    Actuaries and Retirement iii
    Your Own Personal Actuary iv
    Why IRAs? Why Now? iv

Three Conflicts in Your IRA 1
    It Happened to Me 2
    Conflicts in Your IRA 4
    Yes, I'm Talking to You 5
    Outside-the-Box Thinking 6

Conflict No. 1: Growth vs. Security 7
    The Conflict Inherent in Today's Market 8
    Realities of a Volatile Market 9
    The Impact of Volatility 12
    Why It Hurts So Much When the Market Crashes 14
    The Flip Side of the Coin 14

    The Challenge of Low Interest Rates 16

    The Conflict of Growth vs. Security 18

Conflict No. 2: Income vs. Legacy 21

    My Conflicted IRA 22

    Finding the Balance 24

Conflict No. 3: You vs. Uncle Sam 27

    Your Hidden Debt 27

    Your Silent Partner 29

    The Great American Savings Myth 29

    This. Is. Important. 30

    Tax-Efficient Income Planning 30

    The Tax Status of How You Save 31

    Which One is Best? 33

    Will Your Tax Rate be Lower in Retirement? 34

    The Million-Dollar Question 35

    Assuming That Risk 39

    What Does It Mean in Dollars and Cents? 39

    Crunching Numbers 40

    The Cost of Conversion 43

- Which Path to Travel? 44
- Your Three Conflicts 44

From Compromise to Realize 45
- How Do I Define Success? 46
- 7702 48
- IUL 50
- Always Question What You Read 52

Eliminating the Conflict of Growth vs. Security 53
- What's the Worst That Can Happen? 57
- The Money Manager 60

Eliminating the Conflict of Income vs. Legacy 61
- The Four Big Needs in Retirement 61
- Getting Your Money 62
- Your Money, Undiscounted 63
- Help for the Medical Cost of Aging 64
- Legacy for Your Heirs 65

Eliminating the Conflict of You vs. Uncle Sam 67
- Kicking Uncle Sam to the Curb 68
- Brief and to the Point 69

Putting My Money Where My Mouth Is 71

    A Different Kind of Conversion 72

    How Much to Convert? 72

    Confidence in My Choice 74

Too Good to be True? 75

    Truthful Scale 76

    That's What Neil Thought 79

Final Thoughts 83

    Fat-Free Frozen Yogurt 83

    What the Future Holds 85

Determine if IUL Might Be a Good Fit for You 87

    Finding the Right Help 87

    How Can You Decide? 88

    How Much Should You Allocate to This Strategy? 88

    How Should My Advisor and I Evaluate My Current IRA/401(k)? 89

    How Can I Compare Results to an IUL Policy? 89

    If I Choose to Use IUL, How Should I Handle My Taxes? 90

    How Should My IUL Policy Be Structured? 90

> Feel Good About Your Choice 91

Pay It Forward 93
> New Rules for the Next Generation 93

The New Rules of Retirement Saving .... A
> Crisis in America C
> The Old Rules of Retirement Saving .... E
> Three Rules for a Better Future .... F

Rule #1: Know Your Risks I
> Your Three Biggest Risks I

Prologue

I want to tell you my story.

Most financial books you read tell someone else's story. They look at the problems someone else faced, and how the author — our hero! — saved that person from financial doom.

But not this book.

This book is about me.

And my friends.

And my colleagues.

It's a book about how we chose to save for retirement ... and what that choice means now that retirement is on the horizon.

It's a book about what comes next — for me, and likely for you, too.

Help from an Actuary

I'm an actuary.

Yes, that's right. You're about to read a book written by an actuary.

Wait! Don't shut the cover. There's a good reason you should listen to what actuaries have to say about your retirement.

Sure, I know the old stereotypes. What's an actuary? A CPA without the personality. What's a computer? An actuary with a heart.

But the truth is, actuaries are experts in assessing and reducing risk. We use math, statistics, and complex analysis to determine the true risks in a situation, as well as how to minimize them.

I'm here to tell you: Your IRA is full of risks. In fact, saving for the future is one of the most significant financial risks most of us take in our lifetime.

So it makes sense to have an actuary like me to guide you through these risks.

The problem is, most actuaries work for large financial and insurance companies, where they sit in a tall corporate tower, far away from consumers like you. Most actuaries spend their careers helping institutions, not individuals.

I'm here to change that.

Putting Actuarial Expertise on Your Side

Why am I so passionate about bringing actuarial expertise to savers? In 2000, over a cup of coffee, one of my closest friends asked me a question that would change my career.

Until then, I had always worked on the side of institutions: I led product development, created a retail annuity business, and oversaw technology platforms for various insurance carriers. I had even served as CEO of an insurance and annuity company.

But I had never served individual savers. None of the actuaries I knew did.

My friend needed help, so he asked, "Do people like you ever help people like me plan for retirement?"

It was an intriguing question. And, as I thought about it, I couldn't believe the answer was "No."

I've always had an entrepreneurial streak; I love trying things no one has tried before. I realized I could use my actuarial expertise to help individuals instead of corporations.

It became my mission and my passion.

In 2001, I founded Stonewood Financial with the goal of bringing actuarial expertise to everyday savers. While I love helping savers one at a time, this book is my way of helping savers across the country.

Many people have their own doctor, their own CPA, or even their own attorney. So why not have your own actuary to advise you? Through this book, you can.

Actuaries and Retirement

An actuary is someone who uses math and statistics to analyze the financial consequences of risk. You'll find our fingerprints on almost all insurance and financial products. Have you ever wondered how your health insurance company determines your premium each year? At some point in the process of designing the policy, an actuary had to calculate the cost of covering your risk of getting sick, getting injured or dying. If the insurance policy protects your property, such as your home or car, an actuary had to crunch the numbers and predict the odds of your home burning to the ground or your car being involved in an accident.

Wherever you find risk, you'll find actuaries.

Actuaries certainly have a stereotype: We're the geeks of the math world. As one comedian put it: "Actuaries were invented so accountants would have somebody to make fun of."

In a way, we are geeks. Actuaries love numbers. The thing about numbers is they don't lie. They are absolute. If Johnny has an apple stand and sells five apples a day for three days, he will have sold fifteen apples. Case closed. There is no way to spin that. Life may be complex and fraught with a multitude of problems and uncertainty, but logic is simple, and numbers are starkly pure. There is a rare, sweet harmony to math.

The English words "actuary" and "actual" stem from the same Latin root, which connotes "a state of fact" or "that which is real." When analyzed correctly, numbers can tell us much about life, especially its financial side. Take Johnny and his apple stand, for instance. As a merchandiser of fruit, he is no superstar. This had better be a sideline business for the kid, because, at five apples a day, if he has any overhead at all, he is a bankruptcy candidate (of course that may depend on how much he gets per apple). Any financial undertaking held up to the light of analysis by applied actuarial science will have a much better chance of succeeding than one without such benefit. This holds doubly true for retirement planning.

Your Own Personal Actuary

I believe people should have their own actuary the way they have their own doctor, lawyer, or accountant. Actuaries specialize in identifying and reducing risk. And just about everyone's financial portfolio could use help with that.

One of the reasons I founded Stonewood Financial was so I could take the unique science of risk assessment and actuarial problem-solving out of the boardroom and bring it into the living room, so to speak. All of us deal with risk in our financial lives — risk that can be mitigated, or at least prepared for, through actuarial analysis.

Why IRAs? Why Now?

I told you this was a book about me. About my story.

A few years ago, I was helping my adult daughters figure out the best way to save for the future. Frustrated at the outdated advice they were getting, I was moved to write a book: *The New Rules of Retirement Saving*. The book helped younger generations align their savings strategies with the realities of today's market.

One of the hallmarks of that book was a discussion on the pitfalls of traditional tax-deferred retirement accounts, like IRAs and

401(k)s. While writing the book, I couldn't help but feel I had fallen victim to these pitfalls as well.

When my friends and I discuss our retirement plans, none of us do so with affection. We're glad we've saved enough money for a comfortable retirement, but almost all of us feel anxiety about the way we've saved. Was it smart to defer so much in taxes? Do I have enough to live well and leave a legacy? How am I going to keep these funds growing? What if I lose it all in a crash?

The concerns go on and on.

Those concerns gave rise to this book.

In January of 2016, I decided I was finished compromising in my IRA.

I decided I didn't have to accept the limitations of my current strategies.

Most importantly, I decided to quantify the compromises in my IRA — and what they were costing me and my wife as we approach retirement.

While I used my actuarial expertise to identify the impact of these consequences, you don't have to be an actuary to understand the results.

If you've ever felt frustrated with your retirement strategy, this book is for you. I want to show you how I uncovered the ways my IRA was failing me . . . and what I did about it.

CHAPTER ONE

Three Conflicts in Your IRA

We're all part of a cultural movement when it comes to retirement saving.

Most of us have bought into the prevailing ideas on saving for the future. Maybe we heard them from the talking heads on TV, or from a financial advisor or HR professional at work.

But nearly all of us have joined this movement.

Consider: Did you ever stop to think why you save for retirement in an IRA or 401(k)?

Not why you chose the specific account you're in, or why you're invested the way you're invested. I'm talking about why you chose to put the money you're setting aside for the future into a qualified, tax-deferred retirement account.

I'm guessing "chose" is a strong word. Most of us didn't "choose." Our companies, or a financial advisor, or the advice from CNBC chose for us.

At some point, we began believing this was the American way to save. So, we did.

You're not alone. Most of my retirement funds are in 401(k) and IRA accounts. My financially sophisticated friends? You guessed it. They saved in IRAs and 401(k)s, too. For most American savers, qualified accounts are the norm.

Let me be clear at the outset: This book is not here to bash IRAs and 401(k)s. They're an important tool in the toolbox of saving.

1

But, like all choices in life, there are consequences when you choose to save for retirement in a qualified plan. And most of us have never been fully briefed on what those consequences — good and bad — might be.

I wrote this book to talk about those consequences.

Each of us has made compromises to save in a qualified plan. Now, we need to understand them. Only then can we reduce their impact on our retirement funds and, more importantly, our retirement plans.

It Happened to Me

Looking back at my savings experience, it's probably pretty similar to your own.

I graduated from Purdue University in 1972 with a degree in mathematics and physics. I was so eager to start my first job that I skipped my graduation ceremony altogether. While my classmates were tossing their hats in the air, I was settling into a new role as an actuarial student at Travelers Insurance in Hartford, Connecticut.

At that point, saving for retirement was easy: I didn't have to do it personally because my company did it for me. In the 1970s, Travelers had a defined-benefit pension plan, so each year I accrued a portion of my salary that would be paid to me at retirement for the rest of my life. Amazingly, I didn't have to contribute a cent to this plan. It was up to my employer to fully fund it.

If only it had stayed that easy.

By the 1990s, I was CEO of an insurance company called Integrity Life, headquartered in Louisville, Kentucky. Here's where my retirement savings got considerably more complex.

At Integrity, we didn't have a formal pension program. Instead, we saved in what was, at the time, the hot new savings product in America: the 401(k).

Over the years, as I climbed the corporate ladder, I amassed a group of retirement assets that included a small pension and several rollover IRAs. Those IRAs are where my retirement funds have been growing, up and down with the market, as I march on toward retirement.

I'm willing to bet your retirement accounts look similar.

It's an easy bet to make, because the majority of successful U.S. savers have most of their retirement funds in IRAs and 401(k)s.[1]

But here's something I didn't realize as a twenty-five-year-old actuarial student, as a thirty-five-year-old head of insurance product development, or as a forty-five-year-old CEO: I was making a lot of compromises to save in my IRA. And you have, too.

What does that mean? This book will show you.

This book will teach you the three biggest compromises in your IRA, and how you can overcome them to live a happier retirement. Together, we'll transform your thinking around retirement saving, and create a strategy free from compromises.

A word of caution before we begin: As you read this book, you may get a sinking feeling, realizing perhaps you've made some errors while saving. I'm here to tell you not to worry. While you can't go back and make different choices in your past, you do have the power to choose what comes next.

Together, we'll make sure it's the right choice.

---

[1] Sarah Holden and Daniel Schrass. ICI Research Perspective. December 2017. "The Role of IRAs in US Households' Saving for Retirement, 2017."
https://www.ici.org/pdf/per23-10.pdf.

Conflicts in Your IRA

At its core, this is a book about conflict.

What do I mean by conflict? Two needs pulling you in opposite directions. Two goals that are not compatible, where making gains in one area means losing ground in another. I want to eat cake and I want to lose weight. The more cake I eat, the less weight I lose. The more weight I lose, the less cake I can eat. But I can't eat more cake and lose more weight, because there's a conflict inherent in my goals.

Likewise, conflicts have forced you to compromise in your IRA, as you try to balance competing interests.

As innovative Americans, we have figured out how to eliminate conflict from many areas of our lives. What if I want to sleep in but I also want my coffee brewed? No problem. We've created programmable coffee makers so a hot cup is waiting when I get downstairs. How about when I want to join an important meeting in a distant city, but I don't have time to fly across the country to do so? Great! We've created video conferences so I can join in from the comfort of my home office.

When it comes to finances, however, we're still battling a lot of conflicts that have gone unresolved.

Your IRA is home to three major conflicts that act as hurdles to your retirement goals.

- **Growth vs. Protection**: The desire for your funds to grow so you have enough income in retirement, and the desire for your funds to stay protected so they won't be wiped out in the next market crash.
- **Income vs. Legacy**: The desire to use your funds for living expenses in retirement, and the desire to leave your funds as a legacy to your children, grandchildren, or favorite charity.

- **You vs. Uncle Sam:** The desire to use your retirement account as income, and the desire of Uncle Sam to get his portion of the account through taxes.

That's it. Three conflicts.

These three conflicts in your IRA have a bigger impact on your living standards in retirement than almost anything else. Yet, most of us have never tried to overcome them. We assume it's necessary to accommodate them, to plan around them.

I'm here to tell you: It's not.

Yes, I'm Talking to You

I know it's easy to say, "This book isn't for me. I've done a decent job of saving. I'm smart with my money. My account is diversified. I'll be fine."

But the truth is, you are battling these conflicts, too. I'll show you why it matters so much.

Take my client, Andrew. Andrew is a CPA, and he knows numbers. He also knows how to evaluate risk. After one of our meetings, he remarked to me, "You know, when I first met you, I always assumed you were talking about other people. I figured I was smart enough to know what to do with my savings. Heck, I advise my clients on some of the same strategies you're dismissing. But you know what? I needed help, too. I was relying too much on the talking heads and not enough on the level heads."

So, before we begin, let me say: I *am* talking to you. In the pages ahead, you'll see why these three conflicts in your IRA may be the biggest challenge you face in retirement.

Outside-the-Box Thinking

I have one request as we embark on this book's journey together: open your mind and think outside the box. I'm going to give you a different lens through which to view your finances. It's going to feel different from what you've done before. That's good! Because we're here to perform a savings check-up: to make sure conflicts aren't standing in the way of your happy retirement.

When people ask me what I mean by "thinking outside the box," I'm reminded of a story from the early 1900s, where the automobile was just being introduced. A spokesman for Daimler Benz was asked about the future of cars: just how scalable was this new invention? The spokesman thought inside the box. Here was his answer: "There will never be a mass market for motorcars, because there is a limit on the number of chauffeurs available." He was stuck in the box where every car needed a chauffeur. He couldn't see outside the box, where individuals would enjoy driving themselves. He couldn't see the personal automobile.

The same is true with saving today. Too many of us are saying, "I accept the limitations of these strategies, because these strategies are the way people save. It's just the reality of saving."

But, as you've probably guessed by now, we're not going to approach your future inside the box. We're going to take a step back, evaluate where you are today, determine where you want to be, and build a path from one to the other.

Let's get started.

A quick note: Throughout this book, you'll see me using the terms "401(k)," "IRA," "qualified account" and "tax-deferred account" somewhat interchangeably. Regardless of the term, what we're discussing is retirement savings accounts where your funds grow tax-deferred. So, call them what you like — now you'll know what we're talking about in the pages ahead.

CHAPTER TWO

Conflict No. 1: Growth vs. Security

Ever watch CNBC and get overwhelmed with the advice you hear? Or you read USA Today and have trouble sorting out what it all means?

Financial planning can be confusing. It's even harder when the "experts" can't agree.

Here's what we face when we turn on the TV, or read the paper:

"Baby boomers should generally have [up to] 70% of their portfolio in equities." – *USA Today*[2]

So you think: Great. I'll put more of my savings in stocks.

But wait!

"Baby boomers have too much retirement savings in stocks." – *CNN Money*[3]

Hmm. Okay, so, less in stocks.

But wait again!

---

[2] Jeff Reeves. USA Today. Nov. 9, 2015. "The 60/40 stock-and-bond portfolio mix is dead in 2016." https://www.usatoday.com/story/money/personal-finance/2015/11/09/60-40-stock-bond-portfolio-mix-dead-2016/75042316/.

[3] Katie Lobosco. CNN Money. Aug. 14, 2015. "Baby Boomers have too much retirement savings in stocks." http://money.cnn.com/2015/08/14/retirement/retirement-baby-boomers-stocks/index.html.

"Subtract your age from 100 – that's the percent of your portfolio to keep in stocks." – *CNN Money*[4]

This is getting confusing, you think. I'll just fall back on the old tried-and-true advice to keep 60 percent of my portfolio in stocks, and around 40 percent in bonds.

"The 60/40 stock-and-bond portfolio mix is dead." – *Motley Fool*[5]

Oh . . .

See what I mean? No wonder so many savers are confused at best, and fed-up at worst.

The Conflict Inherent in Today's Market

Part of the problem is today's market is filled with conflicts of its own, and that makes allocating your funds very difficult.

Take my client Eddie. Eddie is sixty-six years old and recently retired from one of the largest construction companies in our state. He's done a pretty good job of saving in his company's 401(k) program, but he'll be the first to admit he underestimated just how much income he and his wife need in retirement. He once quipped to me, "I've got grandkids stretching from California to South Carolina. We'll burn through our retirement funds in airfare alone!"

Eddie is faced with a very common problem, one I suspect you struggle with, too.

First, Eddie wants his retirement funds to grow.

Second, Eddie wants his retirement funds to stay safe.

---

[4] CNN Money. 2018. "Ultimate Guide to Retirement." http://money.cnn.com/retirement/guide/investing_basics.moneymag/index7.htm.

[5] Selena Maranjian. The Motley Fool. Dec. 29, 2016. "5 Facts About Stocks Every Baby Boomer Should Know." https://www.fool.com/retirement/2016/12/29/5-facts-about-stocks-every-baby-boomer-should-know.aspx.

While he's saved well, he can't afford the retirement he wants if his 401(k) never grows. Yet, while he needs his account to grow, he can't afford the retirement he wants if his account is wiped out by a stock market crash.

This creates a conflict for Eddie, and for you and me as well.

While Eddie was saving, his account grew by contributions and investment earnings; he had two ways to boost his retirement funds. But now that he's retired, his account can only grow by investment earnings: it can only grow by what it earns in the market. He can't ignore growth while he's retired.

Where can he find that growth?

Let's take a look at Eddie's challenge.

Realities of a Volatile Market

Do you have some of your retirement funds in mutual funds? Target date funds? Stocks? If so, congratulations. You're depending on the stock market for growth.

Traditionally, the stock market is where we've turned for growth. There's nothing wrong with that approach but, as savers, we need to understand what today's market is, and what it is not.

Remember the 1990s? There are a lot of things I don't miss from the 90s. Flip phones that could barely text. Beanie Babies that somehow convinced millions of adults to buy stuffed animals. Windows 95.

But there's one thing I miss from the 90s every day: the stock market.

The 1990s were booming days in the market. You might remember something called "Dart Funds" — these were funds you could invest in where a stockbroker literally threw a dart at a sheet of stocks and invested in whichever ones the dart hit. You know what? Dart funds were making good money! Everything was making good money. The market was going up, up, up.

We all know what happened after the feel-good years of the 90s: the dot-com bubble burst. If you're like me and the majority of Americans, for the last two decades, you've been riding the market roller coaster as we recover and then crash again.

The 2000s started low: From March of 2000 to October of 2002, the NASDAQ lost 78 percent of its value. The S&P 500®, which is an index that economists often use to measure the overall health of the stock market, fell by nearly 40 percent. In a series of months, many people's retirement accounts were severely depleted. A running joke at the time was that 401(k)s had been reduced to 201(k)s.[6,7]

The good news is, the market didn't stay down. From 2002 to 2008, the market recovered. Those were okay years. Most of us were trying to earn back what we had lost in our retirement accounts. The market was helping us along.

Then the real estate bubble burst in 2008 and sent the market crashing again.

Today, the market has recovered. In fact, the S&P 500® is hovering around all-time highs. And, as any financial advisor will tell you, if you rode the wave, you've come out on top. If you didn't get scared and sell when the market was down, if you didn't panic and buy when the market was high, if you just stayed the course, you slowly recovered.

Recently, we've watched volatility return to the market. Most experts, including myself, believe the next big crash isn't a question of if but when. But I'm not here to scare you with talks of the next great crash. Instead, I'm here to help you evaluate what a volatile

---

[6] Multpl.com. March 13, 2018. "S&P 500 Historical Prices by Year."
http://www.multpl.com/s-p-500-historical-prices/table/by-year.

[7] Investing.com. March 13, 2018. "NASDAQ Composite Historical Data."
https://www.investing.com/indices/nasdaq-composite-historical-data.

market means for the equities-exposed portion of your retirement account.

Here's what many people don't realize: So far this century — from 2000 to the end of 2018 — the stock market has seen two bear markets (crashes) and two bull markets (growth periods). That's a LOT of volatility.

If you stayed the course and didn't panic, you've done well. You're reaped the benefits of all-time highs in the market. Right?

Well, not quite.

From 2000 to 2018, the S&P 500® (a measurement of the 500 largest stocks on the exchange, which is what people usually mean when they say "the market") returned an average of 4.8 percent. All that risk — riding the roller coaster through booms and busts — netted you a little less than 5 percent a year. Remember, that's your growth before you pay the fees inside your 401(k) or IRA, and of course before the IRS takes out his portion for taxes.

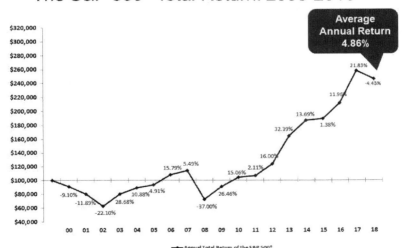

Source: Yahoo Finance GSPC Historical Prices 2019

You might ask yourself: Is 4.8 percent worth all that risk?

The Impact of Volatility

Imagine you had to save during the worst decade in modern U.S. market history. A market so bad you would, on average, lose money every year. A market that saw not just one but TWO crashes that wiped out more than a third of your savings' value.

We feel for our parents and grandparents who lived through that kind of market with the Great Depression. But here's a surprise: their generation isn't the only one that had to work and save during one of the worst markets in history. You did, too.

The years 2000 through 2009 are estimated to be the single worst decade in S&P 500® history. You might have heard it called the "lost decade of investing," because the market that decade ended lower than it started.

How bad was it? For those number geeks like me, this next section will be very exciting. If you're not a numbers person, don't worry — I'll explain what all the numbers mean.

If you had a 401(k) with $100,000 in it, completely invested in the S&P 500®, what would have happened over the first decade of this century? Well, look at the line on the preceding chart marked, "Annual Total Return of the S&P 500®." This represents your account value. The market crashes from 2000 to 2002. It takes you four years to earn back what you've lost, and finally by 2006, you're above water. Then, in 2008, you lose it all again.

You saw some good years. The market was up 28 percent in 2003 and 26 percent in 2009. But you used those big gains to earn back the money you lost when the market dropped. So those gains really didn't reflect forward progress, did they?

In fact, it's even less progress than you think.

Guess what your 401(k) earned, on average, from 2000 through 2009, if it was invested wholly in "the market"? Four percent? Three percent?

The answer may surprise you. It's negative 1 percent. That's right. For the entire decade, you lost about 1 percent on average per year.

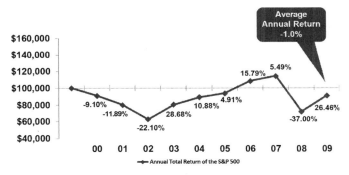

The S&P 500® Total Return: 2000-2009

Source: Yahoo Finance GSPC Historical Prices 2018

That's frightening data when you're trying to grow and protect your retirement savings.

As I mentioned, the experience over the rest of the century hasn't been much better. Remember, from 2000 through the end of 2018, the S&P 500® has returned an average of 4.8 percent per year. Not terrible (at least you didn't lose money), but also not enough to grow your account value in a meaningful way. And, remember, that's your growth before you pay the fees inside your 401(k) or IRA and before you pay taxes.

No one is going to successfully retire on an account that's growing in the very low single digits. You need meaningful growth to fuel your account.

Why It Hurts So Much When the Market Crashes

Here's a very concrete example of why most savers weren't celebrating when the market rose 28 percent in 2003. Below is a chart of the growth needed for recovery when the market drops:

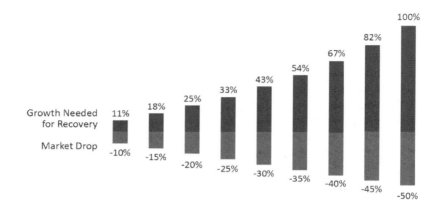

That's right. If the market drops 50 percent, your account needs to grow by 100 percent to make up that loss. So, when the market dropped 22 percent in 2002, and went up 28 percent in 2003, many savers were still under water: They hadn't earned back everything they had lost.

Let's put it another way. You have $10. You lose 50 percent of it. Now you have $5. You grow that money by 50 percent. Now you have $7.50. You're still $2.50 short of where you started.

The Flip Side of the Coin

Right now, you're probably thinking, "Okay, Marty. I get it. The market is volatile. That's why my account is diversified. So what?"

Here's what.

In today's market, to get diversification, you have to give up a lot of growth.

That's a core conflict of your IRA.

My friends and I saved with a mistaken belief: we assumed once we hit age sixty-five, we could put our funds into safer instruments and be done with it. Sure, they wouldn't grow as much in CDs as they did in stocks, but we could still get meaningful growth on our funds while keeping them protected.

Think back to the 1970s and 80s. Perhaps you were like me. When I was in my thirties, I opened a checking account at the local bank in Louisville, Kentucky. It was a basic checking account, a place to deposit my checks (remember when you had to drive to the bank to deposit a check?) and pay my bills (remember when you had to write a check to pay a bill?).

From this account, I was very careful about when I paid my bills. I always waited until the last day possible, and then wrote a check and put it in the mail.

This odd behavior wasn't because I was broke; I had enough money to cover my bills.

Can you guess why I did this?

In 1980, my checking account was earning an interest rate of around 18 percent.

Eighteen percent! I wanted to keep my money in the bank and earning that interest as long as I could.

It's hard to remember back when money could achieve meaningful growth in secure vehicles. It's just not a reality anymore.

Most checking accounts today earn around 0.10 percent. When was the last time you saw a checking account earning interest on the left side of the decimal point? It doesn't happen anymore.

The Challenge of Low Interest Rates

Low interest rates have been a boon for borrowers. Auto loans? Less than 2 percent. Mortgage loans? Less than 6 percent.

But the same low interest rates that make it easy to buy a car or finance a home have made it very challenging to grow wealth safely.

My father owned a children's clothing store in New Albany, Indiana. As a small business owner, he didn't have a pension or corporate plan, so, in retirement he and my mother lived off what he had managed to save and grow on his own. They spent frugally and did what so many retirees of my parent's generation did: largely lived off the interest from CDs.

I used to think I'd live off CD interest in retirement, too. But that's not an attractive option for today's savers. Even five-year CDs are returning just over 2 percent. It's not enough.

If you don't want the volatility of the market, you're stuck with low growth.

That's because most safe alternatives to the stock market rely on interest rates. And low interest rates are here to stay . . . at least in the near term.

Interest rates have been falling steadily since the mid-1980s and are currently near historic lows. These low rates have helped companies afford to hire workers, and workers afford to buy bread, milk, cars, and clothes at prices that aren't pumped up by inflation.

Recently, rates have begun to rise — but only modestly. No one is suggesting we go back to rates we saw in the 80s and 90s anytime soon. Here's one reason why.

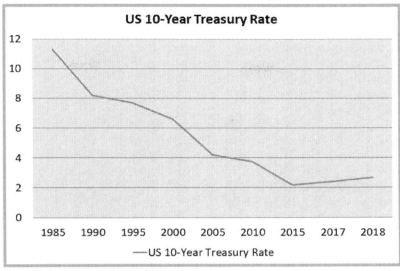

Source: U.S. Treasury – Treasury Yield Rates

The government wants — and needs — low interest rates.

The U.S. government has a big incentive to help keep interest rates low: It reduces Uncle Sam's debt payments. An increasingly large portion of our federal budget each year goes to paying interest on the U.S. debt. In 2010, 6 percent of our federal budget was dedicated to debt service, or around $209 billion. By 2035, the Congressional Budget Office projects debt service will grow to 25 percent of the budget, or around $2.27 trillion. As this book is written, the federal government is borrowing and repaying money at very low interest rates. If those rates rise, so does our national debt. Consider: Between 2011 and 2013, the gross federal debt rose more than $3 trillion. If interest rates had been just 1 percent higher during that time, the government would owe an additional $30 billion in interest each year.

On June 1, 2005, the total national debt was $7,775,753,817,632.01. Ten years later, June 1, 2015, it was

$18,152,841,401,259.20 — more than double.[8] Politicians like to talk about slowing the growth of our national debt, but few hope to reverse the trend altogether. And this suggests interest rates are going to stay relatively low for the foreseeable future.

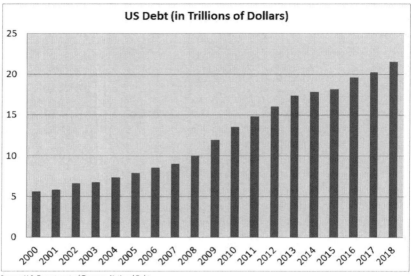

Source: U.S. Department of Treasury, National Debt

So, what does this mean for your retirement account? It's going to be hard to grow your savings significantly in safer vehicles — likely for many years to come.

The Conflict of Growth vs. Security

Here's the first big conflict in your IRA. You can choose growth potential in the market and assume a lot of risk and volatility to do

---

[8] Treasury Direct. "The Debt to the Penny and Who Holds It." http://www.treasurydirect.gov/NP/debt/current

so. Or you can choose security in CDs and money market funds and give up any kind of meaningful growth.

But you can't have growth AND security.

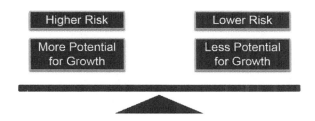

This is often called the "Saver's Dilemma," and it's impacting your IRA today.

You have to compromise because of this conflict: give up some growth to get protection; give up some protection to get growth.

That compromise means your account is growing slower than it could be, and at the same time, your account is less protected than it should be.

This is one of your IRA's key conflicts, and probably the one that sounds most familiar to you. But there are two other conflicts you need to consider as you head to retirement.

CHAPTER THREE

Conflict No. 2: Income vs. Legacy

In the last chapter, we focused on how you might be growing your retirement funds. In this chapter, I want to focus on how you might use your retirement funds.

Not surprisingly, there are conflicts in your IRA here, too.

I have good friends, James and Lynda. They've been blessed with two children and more importantly — as anyone my age will tell you — four beautiful grandchildren.

James and Lynda are planning to retire in two years, when they reach seventy.

When we get together for dinner at their house, one of their favorite things to do is update my wife and me on their plans for retirement. They're building a swimming pool in their backyard for when the grandkids visit in the summer. They're planning to spend two months every winter out in Phoenix, where their son and his wife live.

The point is, James and Lynda are going to need a good amount of income to make their retirement plans a reality.

Thankfully, they're in a good place: they've saved well.

But over dinner one night, the conversation turned to inheritances. Unwittingly, during the course of the discussion, James uncovered a big conflict in his retirement account.

James' family grew up at the lower end of the middle class. When his dad passed away, there wasn't much need for a will, because there wasn't much to pass on to his kids. His dad had sold his house to help cover his nursing home care and had gone through most of his savings in pursuit of the same.

But James built a good career as an attorney in Louisville. While he never expected an inheritance from his dad, he wanted to leave one to his kids.

The reality James faces — the same reality I face and one I bet you do, too — is that we have one pot of money. We've saved, and now it's a question of how that money will be distributed. Do I use it while I'm living, as income? Or does it go to my kids once I'm no longer here, as an inheritance?

This creates a big conflict in your IRA.

My Conflicted IRA

When I think about my IRA, I know I'm going to need it for four things:

First, and most obviously, I'll need to use it for income to cover everyday expenses.

While my wife will tell you I'll never retire (I'm not sure she wants me puttering around our house, anyway), at some point, I'm going to either work less or stop working altogether. So, when my income drops or disappears, I'm going to need money every month to buy groceries and pay our cable bill.

This is why most of us started an IRA or 401(k) in the first place: for retirement income in the future.

But there are three other ways I'll likely use my IRA.

One is for the medical costs associated with aging. After all, expensive medical bills aren't factored into our budgets, but they're a reality for many of us in retirement.

It may surprise you to learn a healthy sixty-five-year-old couple could spend nearly $400,000 out of pocket on medical expenses in retirement.[9] We're not talking about spare change. My IRA will have to help cover costs as my wife and I age: in-home nurses, medical procedures, physical therapy, medicines. It adds up — potentially to the tune of $400,000.

Next, I will likely have unplanned expenses. My house needs a new roof. My wife needs a new car. The basement floods. We all have emergency needs eventually, needs we can't predict and don't necessarily budget for in our annual income. My IRA will have to support some of those as well.

These first three demands on my IRA — income, medical expenses, emergencies — are all money I'll be spending.

But if you're like me and my friend James, you'll also want to leave a legacy for your children, grandchildren, or charity.

That means your IRA also has to cover your legacy needs.

I have two adult daughters and four grandchildren. While I've worked with my daughters throughout their lives to be good savers and plan for their own futures, I'd still like to leave something to them when I'm no longer here. My wife and I have also made commitments to charities that are important to us: religious institutions, educational institutions, hunger organizations.

If you want to leave a legacy, your IRA is pulling double duty. And there's a big conflict embedded in that.

---

[9] HealthView Services. Aug. 31, 2017. "2015 Retirement Health Care Costs Data Report." http://www.hvsfinancial.com/2017/08/31/closing-the-retirement-health-care-costs-planning-gap/.

Finding the Balance

My IRA may end up being used like this:

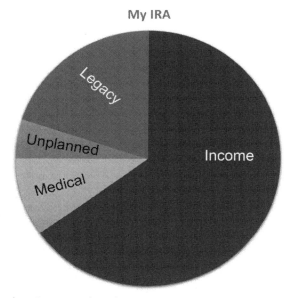

But here's what I realized: my IRA — and your IRA, too — is a zero-sum game.

That means the more money I use as income, the less money I have as inheritance for my kids. And the more inheritance I want to leave my kids, the less of my IRA I can spend as income.

As an actuary, I'm trained on life expectancy and risk. When I counsel people on saving, I emphasize an important reality: The risk to your loved ones is dying too soon, but the risk to your savings is living too long.

Medical advances are helping people live longer and fuller lives — many of us will live well into our nineties or even beyond.

Life expectancy is nearly ten years longer today than it was when I started saving in the 1970s. That means we're going to use a lot more income while we're living, and potentially have less to pass on as inheritance.

No matter how long you live or how much you spend, your IRA is still a zero-sum game. It's one pot of money, and you face conflicts on how to divide it up.

So, conflict No. 2 pits you against your heirs: How much will you spend, and how much will you be able to pass on?

Of course, whether you plan to use your funds as income or legacy, there's still a big chunk of that money you won't get to keep, and that brings us to conflict No. 3.

CHAPTER FOUR

Conflict No. 3: You vs. Uncle Sam

You've probably heard of Dave Ramsey before. He's an author, radio host, TV star, and popular purveyor of financial advice. If you've ever listened to his show, you know his most famous mantra: get out of debt!

Ramsey encourages Americans to pay off their credit card debt, car loans, medical bills – even their mortgages.

In general, it's good advice. Americans could use a lot less debt.

But I'm always alarmed Ramsey overlooks one of the biggest debts nearly every American carries.

Your Hidden Debt

I call this your hidden debt, since so few of us realize we carry it.

You may have paid off your mortgage. Student loans may be decades in your past. You may own your car and pay off your credit card bill each month. But if you've saved for retirement in a 401(k) or IRA, you are NOT debt free.

So, what's your hidden debt?

The taxes you owe in your qualified account.

My client Dave never considered his hidden debt.

Dave has $760,000 in a 401(k). When I first met him, he was laser-focused on income: he and wife needed $100,000 a year in income for the retirement lifestyle they desired. He wanted to know the best way to manage and protect his $760,000 so that, along with Social Security and his wife's pension, they could meet their income goal.

But Dave forgot about his hidden debt. He believed his IRA was worth $760,000.

It wasn't.

Dave's tax liability is around 25 percent. So, when he withdraws $50,000 from his IRA, he only gets to keep $37,500. The other $12,500? That's the taxes he owes. That's his debt payment to the IRS.

Put another way, Dave is indebted to the IRS (and its state and local partners) for around 25 percent of Dave's retirement funds. While he was saving, Dave got a tax deduction on his 401(k) contribution every year. It was like a loan he didn't have to repay anytime soon. But now, as Dave gets ready to retire, he'll start to repay that loan.

Why don't most of us think about our hidden debt? Because it doesn't impact us now. When you buy a house on mortgage, you live in the house every day and make your mortgage payments each month. But with your IRA, you're not using the money until years in the future, and the debt isn't immediately clear.

It's about to become clear.

Like Dave, when you begin accessing funds from your IRA or 401(k), you begin paying back your debt to the IRS.

And it gets worse. Because in truth, you're paying back that debt with interest. After all, you deferred taxes only on your IRA contributions. Now, you'll be paying taxes on your IRA contributions AND all the growth that's occurred in your account. The IRS is taking its cut of your principle and your earnings.

Your Silent Partner

It's time to start thinking of the IRS as the silent partner in your IRA.

Just how big of a silent partner? That depends on how big your tax liability is.

In Dave's case, around $190,000 of his IRA isn't his.

So, when Dave is planning for his retirement income, he doesn't really have $760,000 to use. He has a base of $570,000 that he'll be able to spend as income.

The Great American Savings Myth

This is the basis for what I call the Great American Savings Myth: American savers believe the money in their qualified accounts is theirs to spend.

But it's not. Not all of it, anyway. When you look at your IRA or 401(k) statement, your account isn't worth the number on that piece of paper.

Have you fallen victim to the Great American Savings Myth? Don't feel ashamed! I did, too. And so has the vast majority of our peers. Most of us are taught to think this way. We focus on the number that shows up on our statement, but not how much of that number we'll get to keep. It's how we've been trained to look at our retirement savings.

The Great American Savings Myth may be one of the costliest assumptions many of us will make in our entire savings experience. And in this chapter, we'll look at the importance of approaching your retirement accounts with open eyes and a complete understanding of how the choices you make today will impact your income in retirement.

I suspect the tax status of your retirement accounts has been an afterthought until now. This chapter will change that.

This. Is. Important.

If there is only one thing you take from this book, this is it: you MUST incorporate tax planning into your retirement planning. It is no longer enough to ensure your retirement funds are diversified when it comes to asset allocation. They must also be diversified when it comes to tax status.

Tax-Efficient Income Planning

In the financial industry, a focus on tax diversification for retirement assets is often called "tax-efficient income planning." And if you're not working with a financial advisor who's an expert in this area, you should be. Tax-efficient planning looks at the tax makeup of your portfolio and tries to get you the most *after-tax* income for each dollar of your savings.

We'll explore what this means in the pages ahead.

But for now, I want to offer a warning: savers who fail to plan with taxes in mind risk paying hundreds of thousands of dollars too much in taxes when they're retired. In the next sections, I'll show you why.

Before we go on, I want to make something clear: I'm not a CPA. I'm not a tax professional of any kind. I'm an actuary, and a saver. Additionally, I don't know your individual situation. That's one of the limitations of a book. You should consult a tax professional about any specific questions you have.

But what I am qualified to do is change the way you think about taxes when it comes to your IRA or 401(k). And that's what this chapter is all about.

The Tax Status of How You Save

There are three main tax structures you can save under for retirement.

Taxable Saving

Taxable saving means you don't get a tax deduction for the funds you put in the account, AND you pay taxes on your earnings each year. For example, think about your savings account at the bank. Each year, you pay taxes on your income and then put some of that income into your savings account. When you file your taxes, the interest earned on your account is subject to taxation. So, every year, Uncle Sam is taking a small cut. The majority of retirement savings are not held in taxable accounts, though most people have some long-term savings in this kind of structure. For example, many brokerage accounts are taxable. Usually, real estate is taxable; so are typical CDs and money market accounts you can get at the bank. Unless you acquire these types of assets through a qualified retirement plan, they are taxable.

- **Pluses**: These may be the only option for some of your funds, or some of the account types you want.
- **Minuses**: Paying taxes on earnings each year reduces the amount growing by the tax bill, so you have less money compounding.

Tax-Deferred Saving

This is the most common way to save for retirement. Tax-deferred accounts work like this: you do not pay any taxes on your contributions today. In the future, when you access the funds, you pay taxes on your contributions and all the earnings associated with the account. This is how traditional 401(k)s and IRAs work. Most of us have a good portion of our retirement savings in tax-deferred vehicles.

- **Pluses**: You can deduct contributions in the year you make them, lowering your overall taxable income for that year. For some people, their tax rate could be lower in retirement than it is today, making it wise to defer paying those taxes.
- **Minuses**: All the money you grow from the day you start saving until retirement will be taxed. If your $20,000 grows to $100,000, you will owe taxes on the entire $100,000 when you withdraw it. Additionally, you accept the risk of unknown tax rates in the future, particularly if rates rise.

Tax-Free Saving

Tax-free accounts work like this: you pay taxes on your income before you put it in the account. But, in the future, when you access your funds, no additional taxes are due: you don't pay taxes on your contributions (already paid) OR your earnings (because they have grown tax-free). This savings strategy is growing rapidly in popularity. It's how Roth IRAs and Roth 401(k)s work.

- **Pluses**: All accumulation in the account is tax-free. If your $20,000 grows to $100,000, you'll never pay taxes on the $80,000 gain. Many professionals do not expect to be in a lower tax bracket in retirement, so it makes

sense for them to pay taxes upfront. You are also protected from future changes in tax rates and tax law.
- **Minuses**: You cannot deduct contributions to lower your taxes during your contribution years. There may be limitations on how much you can contribute to these types of plans each year.

Which One is Best?

I believe most savers today need to be growing and accessing at least a portion of their retirement funds tax free. It's certainly the best approach for me and my wife, and this book will help you determine if it's the best approach for you, too.

Many people forget the tax deferral in an IRA or 401(k) is not a gift. Sure, you get a deduction the year you contribute to a qualified account. But it's not like taking a mortgage deduction or child deduction on your taxes. Those deductions lower your tax bill today, with no repercussions in the future. But the deductions you get for contributing to a 401(k) or IRA today come with strings attached: they require you to pay back those taxes (with the interest earned) in the future. That's why the accounts are called tax-*deferred* accounts. You're not doing away with your tax liability; you're just deferring it to the future.

In essence, the government is giving you a very expensive loan to avoid paying taxes today. A loan you have to pay back with interest.

There are two reasons I believe many savers — including myself — are better off saving at least a portion of their retirement funds tax-free. One is theoretical, and one is actuarial.

Will Your Tax Rate be Lower in Retirement?

The first reason is theoretical. The benefit of tax-deferred saving is largely based on deferring your taxes at a higher rate, and then paying your taxes at a lower rate.

I think of this as my parents' tax strategy.

As I mentioned, my dad was a small business owner, managing a regional chain of children's clothing stores. He made a solidly middle-class living and worked hard to do it every day. When he retired, he and my mom really cut back. They'd buy generic-brand sodas instead of Coke. They didn't travel much, and while they occasionally ate out, it was mostly meeting friends for senior discounts at Denny's or coffee at McDonald's. Like many retirees in their generation, they were thrifty and did more with less. In that way, they were able to lower their tax liability in retirement, because they used less income in retirement.

But that's not the way today's baby boomers think. My wife and I are a perfect example.

When we retire, we plan to travel extensively. My wife loves castles and wants a return visit to Scotland. We both bike and enjoy bicycle trips to Europe — which we'll do as long as we can. In retirement, we also plan to spend more time dining out and trying new experiences. We recently bought a new house in a trendy part of Louisville; it's within walking distance of a variety of shops, restaurants, and the local nightlife. In fact, my daughters joke we're going to have more fun in retirement than we did in college.

Most people like me don't want to cut back in retirement. We don't want to live more thrifty lives, counting every dollar with no breathing room. We want to maintain our pre-retirement lifestyle, and to do that we'll need to maintain our pre-retirement income level.

This is part of why I believe most Americans are not going to be in a significantly lower tax bracket once they retire. To preserve our lifestyles, we'll have to preserve our incomes.

But this is only one aspect of determining if tax-deferred saving or tax-free saving is right for you. The tax bracket I'm in is half the story; the other half is how much of my income is subject to that bracket.

The Million-Dollar Question

As a general trend, do you think taxes are going up or down in the future?

I've asked that question a thousand times in the past year, and nearly every single person has answered the same way: Up.

Here's why so many of us feel that way.

The federal debt is rising and rising. In the last chapter, we talked about how this was a good incentive for the government to keep interest rates low. But it's also a good incentive for the government to grow taxes.

How bad is it?

In 2013, analysts were excited that the federal deficit that year would be the first deficit in five years to increase by less than $1 trillion.[10]

It was considered great news that our deficit was *only* going to grow by $1 trillion. One TRILLION dollars. A one with 12 zeroes: $1,000,000,000,000.

Thirty years ago, no one even spoke in terms of trillions. That wasn't even a unit of measurement most people knew. Billions used

---

[10] Congressional Budget Office. Feb. 5, 2013. "The Budget and Economic Outlook: Fiscal Years 2013 to 2023." http://www.cbo.gov/publication/43907.

to be a mind-blowing amount of debt. And now we measure in trillions.

Someone has to help pay for this debt, and that someone is U.S. taxpayers.

So, let's talk about ways your taxes could go up — now and in retirement.

There are four primary ways your taxes could rise.

No. 1: The government raises tax rates.

Here's the most common way people think taxes rise. Today, a couple making $200,000 pays a 24 percent marginal tax rate on their income. But Congress could change the rules, and in the future that same couple making that same $200,000 could pay a 30 percent tax rate on their income.

In fact, we know taxes are going up in the future, because they are artificially low today. In December 2017, Congress passed the most sweeping overhaul of the U.S Tax Code we've seen in nearly thirty years. It reduced the marginal tax rate for many savers, and because of it, many of us today are in lower tax brackets than we were a few years ago.

But those tax brackets don't last forever! They are a temporary adjustment. As Congress often does, it included sunset provisions in the bill. That means, in the future, the tax cuts expire and revert back to the old levels. In fact, most household tax provisions in the new law sunset in 2025. So, you can plan on tax rates rising in the near future unless Congress acts again to keep them low.

Married, Filing Jointly[11]		
Income	Previous Tax Rate	New Tax Rate
$160,000	28%	22%
$250,000	33%	24%
$500,000	39.6%	35%

No. 2: You make more money.

This is a good problem to have, but one that's not terribly likely to occur once you're retired. Today, you're making $100,000 and paying at the 24 percent tax rate. Next year, you're making $200,000 and paying at the 32 percent tax rate. You're making more money, which is great. But you owe more of it to the government as well.

No. 3: Your deductions are eliminated.

Most people can take a variety of tax deductions. For example, if you pay interest on your mortgage, it's usually tax-deductible. But there's a trend in Washington toward taking away those deductions. Put another way, you could have to pay taxes on a larger part of your income. Call it what you wish, but that's a tax increase.

Let's say you make $80,000, but with deductions and credits your total taxable income becomes $72,000. If those deductions go away, you'll essentially have $8,000 more on which you must now pay taxes. That means you could owe $2,000 extra in taxes.

---

[11] U.S. Internal Revenue Service via the Motley Fool. Dec. 29, 2017. "Your Complete Guide to the 2018 Tax Changes." https://www.fool.com/taxes/2017/12/29/your-complete-guide-to-the-2018-tax-changes.aspx.

No. 4: The government taxes more things.

This is another way the government could tax more of your income. Here's a good example. You don't pay Social Security taxes on every dollar you make. There's a limit, called the "maximum taxable earnings." In 2014, the Social Security taxable earnings cap was $117,000. That meant, if you made $90,000, you paid Social Security taxes on all of it, but if you made $120,000, you paid taxes only on the first $117,000. In that case, $3,000 would not be subject to Social Security tax.

Things changed in 2015, however. The maximum taxable earnings for Social Security increased to $118,500. So, if you earned $120,000 in 2015, you no longer avoided taxes on $3,000, only on $1,500. You pay more in taxes despite your income staying the same.[12]

If you don't believe there are sneaky ways your taxes could go up, consider one of my clients, Mattie. Mattie owns a catering company. She's very successful, catering not only weddings and special events but a growing number of corporate lunches and dinners in our community.

Several years ago at tax time, Mattie discovered she owed $1,266 more in taxes than she planned. She didn't have more income than the previous year, and she knew her tax bracket hadn't changed. There had been no new tax increases announced by Congress. She was more than a little confused.

Her accountant cleared it up for her: in the Affordable Care Act (otherwise known as Obamacare), there was a provision to increase the threshold for Social Security taxes. Mattie now owed Social Security taxes on a large part of her income, and, accordingly, her tax bill was higher.

---

[12] Patrick J. Purcell. Social Security. December 2015. "Income Taxes on Social Security Benefits." https://www.ssa.gov/policy/docs/issuepapers/ip2015-02.html.

Since 2012, the federal government has raised taxes on capital gains and dividends, Medicare surtax, payroll taxes and taxes for higher earners. That's in the last few years alone.

Assuming That Risk

When you save tax-deferred, you are assuming the risk of future tax rates, deductions and exemptions. You accept a large unknown in your retirement account and, accordingly, in your retirement income. When it comes right down to it, how confident are you that the tax environment will stay the same over the next thirty to forty years? I'm betting not very confident.

What Does It Mean in Dollars and Cents?

Okay, so perhaps I've convinced you that, in theory, your taxes may not be going down in retirement. But what does that mean in dollars and cents?

I'll show you.

I'm going to take you through a process I developed for myself.

About a year ago, I was sitting around thinking about my IRA. (Yes, this is a real thing that actuaries do.) I had become more and more interested in tax strategies in retirement, particularly in strategies around Roth conversions. A Roth conversion is when you convert your tax-deferred account (like an IRA) into a tax-free account, like a Roth IRA. Usually, this means the saver withdraws funds from the qualified account, pays the taxes on those funds, and then deposits the funds into a tax-free Roth account.

The idea had always interested me, primarily because my wife and I don't expect to be in a lower tax bracket when we retire.

But despite my interest in the concept of Roth conversions, I found it hard to evaluate the information I was reading. After all, most of it was theoretical, and I'm a numbers guy.

I knew tax-deferred saving in an IRA or 401(k) could pack a big tax bill in retirement. I hear my friends and clients grumble about the taxes they're paying to actually use their money in retirement. In fact, my brother-in-law once remarked his IRA was basically a big ticking tax bomb.

But how much in taxes are we really talking about?

And how does it compare to the Roth approach?

Like any good actuary, I opened up Excel and started calculating.

My goal was to determine the total amount of taxes I was going to pay from my IRA from now until I died.

I knew it would be high. But I was absolutely blown away by what I found.

Crunching Numbers

Like many savers, my retirement assets are spread across more than one account. When I went to evaluate my total tax liability, I decided to just focus on one account: an IRA with around $700,000 in it.

I looked at that $700,000 and thought of all the places it would be taxed.

First, I used a few assumptions. I assumed I would have a 25 percent total tax liability (state and local) both now and in retirement. Next, I assumed my IRA would grow at an annual, pre-tax rate of 5 percent. Because I wanted to determine the maximum in taxes my IRA could potentially generate, I also decided I wouldn't spend the income I took out of the account, but rather place it in a taxable account earning an after-tax return of 4 percent. Since I wanted to see how much tax I would pay over my lifetime, I assumed I passed away at age ninety.

Pretty conservative assumptions.

I think you'll be as amazed by the results as I was.

Let's look at all the places my IRA money could be taxed as I use it, and then we'll add it up and determine the total tax liability of my IRA.

- My IRA will be taxed when I withdraw funds, either for income or as required minimum distributions (RMDs). As you may know, at age seventy-and-one-half, the IRS requires you to withdraw a minimum amount from your IRA each year. Why? Because you've built up a lot of tax-deferral in your account, and the IRS wants to collect its tax money. It requires you to withdraw (and pay taxes on) a set minimum amount each year, which is calculated as a percent of your account value based on your life expectancy. (If you don't withdraw your RMD, you will be subject to a penalty tax of up to *half* of your missed RMD — Uncle Sam is not playing around.)
- My IRA funds will be taxed when I reinvest them in a taxable account. I'll show you the same example with these funds spent as income next, but for now remember I'm taking the funds and putting them in a taxable money market account.
- My IRA value will be taxed when I die, and the remaining funds are passed to my heirs. Remember, unlike estate taxes, income taxes are due when funds are withdrawn from a qualified account. So, if you leave your spouse or children your remaining IRA value, they will have to pay income tax when accessing those funds. For this analysis, I've assumed all taxes on my remaining IRA account balance are paid if I happen to pass away at age ninety. If my heirs hold them in the tax-deferred

account beyond that, the situation is even worse than the following analysis, as the additional investment earnings would also be taxed.

Here's what it would look like for my $700,000 IRA:

RMD Analysis on Martin's Qualified Accounts (with reinvested RMDs)	
Assuming a 25% tax liability, 5% pre-tax growth with equivalent reinvestment growth	
Receive RMDs to age 90	Per IRS rules
Total taxes paid on RMDs	$221,223
Taxes paid on growth of reinvested RMDs	$90,714
Taxes paid by heirs on remaining IRA value at death (age 90)	$142,587
TOTAL TAXES PAID	**$455,524**

That's a total of $455,524 — on my $700,000 IRA!

What this tells me is that nearly everything I've done to this point — forty-plus years of saving and all the associated growth — has just been to pay off my future tax bill.

Now, if I had used my RMDs as income rather than reinvesting them, my tax bill would be lower, but still incredibly high relative to the size of my account.

RMD Analysis on Martin's Qualified Accounts (with spent RMDs)	
Assuming a 25% tax liability, 5% pre-tax growth	
Receive RMDs to age 90	Per IRS rules
Total taxes paid on RMDs	$221,223
Taxes paid by heirs on remaining IRA value at death (age 90)	$143,587
TOTAL TAXES PAID	**$364,810**

If I use the proceeds as income, I would still pay $364,810 in taxes — more than *half* of my current IRA value.

The Cost of Conversion

The other thing I evaluated was the tax cost of converting my $700,000 IRA to a Roth IRA. For this calculation, I didn't need an Excel spreadsheet.

If I withdrew $700,000 and paid 25 percent in taxes on the withdrawal, I would pay $175,000 in taxes. And then I would be done. So, through age ninety, I would owe $175,000 in taxes.

Now, of course, when I withdrew the $700,000, I might push myself into a higher tax bracket with all that income. More likely, I would spread the withdrawals out over several years to avoid that. But, conceptually, I'm looking at around $175,000 in taxes to convert my IRA.

Taxes on a Roth Conversion	
Assuming a 25% tax liability, 5% pre-tax growth	
Roth conversion	Per IRS rules
Total taxes paid on conversion	$175,000
Taxes paid on Roth account growth	$0
Taxes paid by heirs on remaining Roth value at death (age 90)	$0
TOTAL TAXES PAID	**$175,000**

There's nothing I can do about the $175,000 in taxes. The IRS is going to get that amount no matter what. But there is something I can do about the projected $280,000 more I'll pay if I keep my funds in my IRA. And that was a wake-up call for me.

Which Path to Travel?

I think of it like a highway with two exits. On one exit, I pay a $175,000 toll right now, and then can get to my destination without paying anything else. On the other exit, I stop at tollbooth after tollbooth until I've paid $455,524 to get to my destination.

When I thought about it like this, it was an easy decision.

Why hadn't this occurred to me before?

Because no one had ever quantified my IRA's tax bill before.

But now I know. And now you do, too.

Your Three Conflicts

So, there you have them: the three biggest conflicts in your IRA.
- Growth vs. Security
- Income vs. Legacy
- You vs. Uncle Sam

I could end the book here, and you would still be more informed than most American savers.

But, as you can guess, my story doesn't end here. As an actuary, it wasn't enough for me to simply quantify the conflicts in my IRA. I wanted to eliminate them, as well.

In the chapters that follow, I'm going to share how I've done that.

I'm going to tell you what I did . . . with *my* IRA.

CHAPTER FIVE

From Compromise to Realize

We've discussed how the conflicts in your IRA have forced you to compromise.

Compromising in your IRA means you've had to give up something on both sides to address the conflict.

So, you've given up some growth potential to gain more security: rather than having your funds earning at the market rate, you've had to keep some of your funds in more conservative, lower-yielding options.

You've given up some income potential to gain more legacy, or vice versa: since you're dealing with a zero-sum game, every dollar you use for income is one less you can leave as legacy.

You've given up a lot of your account value to Uncle Sam in taxes: you've compromised how much you'll get by ensuring the government gets its required portion.

I don't know about you, but I wanted to do something more than compromise. I didn't like the idea of giving up so much to get just some of what I wanted and needed.

I wanted to realize the full potential of my retirement, not compromise it.

So where did I start?

With one simple question.

How Do I Define Success?

When I was earning my Master of Business Administration degree back in the 1980s, a popular notion was "defining success." This was the process of answering one simple question: what does our experience look like if we're successful in what we're trying to achieve?

One winter evening, after everyone else had left the office, I sat down and considered this question. If I was trying to stop compromising and start realizing, what would my retirement plan look like? What would it deliver in retirement?

I took out a pen and a legal pad and started to jot things down. Here's what I ultimately decided:

- **The opportunity for meaningful growth.** My account must be able to grow at a meaningful rate, so I have ample funds in retirement.
- **Protection when the market drops.** My account can't be negatively impacted when the market drops. If (when) we have another 2000 or 2008, my account should hold its value.
- **Tax-free income in retirement.** As you probably noticed in Chapter 4, I have become a firm believer in the importance of tax-free funds.
- **Ability to support the income my wife and I need.** Of course, income levels are related to savings levels. But I want to maximize the amount of income I can withdraw each year.
- **A meaningful legacy** to leave my children and grandchildren, so the things that matter most to us will be taken care of when my wife and I are no longer here.

Once I knew what success would look like, I set about determining where I could put my savings to deliver all five goals.

	401(k) / IRA	Roth IRA/ Roth 401(k)	Savings Account	Money Market Fund	Brokerage Account
Meaningful Growth	✓	✓			✓
Protection from Bad Markets			✓	✓	
Tax-Free Income in Retirement		✓			
High Income Levels from Account Balance	Possibly	Possibly			Possibly
A Meaningful Legacy					

As you can see, I found some options that could achieve some of my goals. And for some options, there was the possibility to achieve more of my goals. But I wasn't satisfied with risking my retirement on possibility. I wanted something more concrete.

And that's when I turned to an unlikely place: The U.S. Tax Code.

I Was Looking in the Wrong Part of the Tax Code

Have you ever wondered where the 401(k) got its name?

It's named after a section of the U.S. tax code. Section 401, subsection k of Title 26 of the U.S. Tax Code, to be exact. This section enables individuals to save funds for retirement, with certain restrictions, in a tax-deferred manner.

That's it. The section basically says, for certain retirement funds, you can deduct your contributions in the year you save in exchange for paying taxes on both those contributions and the investment earnings when you withdraw the funds.

It's a funny realization. In truth, what you and I think of as 401(k)s are just savings vehicles that use a certain portion of our tax code. Basically, they're tax shopping carts. You can load up mutual funds, bonds and other financial instruments into your 401(k) shopping cart and they'll receive a particular tax status as long as you keep them in the cart.

IRAs work the same way. They are also just shopping carts given a certain tax treatment by the government.

But here's something many of us forget, or perhaps never knew: Section 401 subsection k is not the only part of the tax code that delivers tax benefits to a given savings approach. In fact, there are many parts of the tax code under which you can house your savings.

In this book, I want to introduce you to Section 7702.

7702

Meet Section 7702 of the U.S. Tax Code.

Section 7702 has been available for saving for years. In fact, it well predates Section 401(k). Only recently has its use become more widespread, as people like you have realized the large deficiencies in Section 401(k).

Here's what a properly structured 7702 plan can deliver:
- Growth when the market is up
- Protection when the market drops
- Tax-free income in retirement
- Additional funds for your legacy
- All at a competitive cost

Sounds great, right?

But what exactly is a 7702 plan?

Life Insurance. Yes, Life Insurance.

Wait, don't close this book!

I know, life insurance isn't what you were expecting me to discover as the cure for the conflicts in my IRA. Frankly, I didn't expect it, either. In fact, I almost wrote it off. After all, I was sixty-six years old. Life insurance is usually marketed to younger people.

But, as an actuary who has made his career in the insurance industry, I knew the benefits of life insurance. In fact, as I discuss in my previous book, I had helped my daughter research and come to the decision that certain kinds of life insurance were the right approach for her and her husband to save for retirement.

But, despite everything I knew, I almost overlooked it as a solution for myself. I want to stop you from making that same mistake.

First, let's talk about life insurance. The number 7702 refers to the part of the U.S. Tax Code that enables funds inside a life insurance policy to accumulate (or grow) tax-free, and provide a death benefit to heirs tax-free as well.

But saying life insurance is good for saving is like saying stocks are good for saving. There are too many different kinds, features and benefits to make a universal statement. Some are clearly better than others.

I assume you're not an actuary. So, you probably don't want to evaluate every kind of insurance on the market and determine the best one for saving.

Thankfully, I am an actuary, and I've done it for you. Here's what you need to know.

IUL

IUL. These three letters just may change the entire way you approach your retirement savings.

Section 7702 existed for years before people really started taking advantage of it. While the tax code allowed individuals to save in life insurance policies, the life insurance products weren't very good for saving.

That all started to change in the early 1990s, with a new breed of life insurance product designed specifically to help people save and grow their funds, while also getting death protection.

That revolution was IUL.

IUL stands for "indexed universal life," a very flexible form of permanent life insurance that is often used as a savings vehicle.

I know a lot about IUL. In fact, in the early 1980s, I was head of product development for Capital Holding, an insurance and annuity company. At that time, a new concept was brewing in the life insurance industry: universal life, a more flexible form of permanent life insurance. While many research papers had been written about the concept, no one had actually gone to market with a product yet.

I decided Capital Holding would be one of the first companies to do so.

My team and I worked tirelessly to create and launch a UL product. While we weren't the first product to market, we were close (another carrier beat us by a month). So, while I can't claim to have invented UL (like Al Gore and the internet), I can say I was there at the beginning.

But even with everything I knew about IUL and UL, it hadn't occurred to me to use it as a savings vehicle myself. After all, most of my funds were in IRAs. For too long, I had bought into the Great American Savings Myth on tax-deferred savings. I had been an enthusiastic promoter of IUL for my daughters, yet I hadn't stopped to consider it for myself.

When I did, it all became clear. This was how I could stop compromising and start realizing.

That's because IUL delivers a package of four benefits no other savings vehicle can:

- Tax-free income in retirement
- The power of indexing to grow and protect your funds
- Access to your funds with no market-value adjustment
- A true death benefit for your heirs

We'll look at these benefits in depth over the next few chapters. When I updated my chart to include IUL, the picture was clear.

	401(k) / IRA	Roth IRA/ Roth 401(k)	Savings Account	Money Market Fund	Broker Account	IUL
Meaningful Growth	✓	✓			✓	✓
Protection from Bad Markets			✓	✓		✓
Tax-Free Income in Retirement		✓				✓
High Income Levels from Account Balance	Possibly	Possibly			Possibly	✓
A Meaningful Legacy						✓

Always Question What You Read

Anyone who knows me will tell you: I question everything. It's like the old newspaper reporter advice: if your mother tells you she loves you, check it out.

"Trust, but verify," is my mantra and it should be yours, too.

This means you should ask lots of questions, and aim to answer the big one: does what I'm hearing bring value to me?

Now, I'll admit, it's a little hard to raise your hand and ask a question while you're reading a book. But I know you're smart, and I know you want to do the right thing with your retirement funds. Otherwise, why would you be reading a book on removing compromise from your retirement plan?

So, as I walk you through the benefits of this savings approach, check in with yourself and see if they solve the conflicts in your own savings account. You'll be surprised with the answer you find.

CHAPTER SIX

Eliminating the Conflict of Growth vs. Security

One of the biggest conflicts in your IRA is between growth and security. Just look at your asset allocation. You are constantly giving up growth for security, and security for growth. In many savings vehicles, when the market is up you make money and when it crashes you lose money. Otherwise, you just slog along at a growth rate far below what you need to accomplish.

It's a terrible choice, but one we're so used to making that most of us never stop to question it. Of COURSE we can't have growth and security. By definition, in today's market, gaining one requires giving up the other.

IUL overcomes this through indexing.

The *indexed* part of indexed universal life explains how interest is credited to a policy. This technique lets you grow your money when the market is up but protects your money when the market drops. It's a "best of both worlds" approach. What's even better? It's pretty simple to understand.

In indexing, you capture a portion of the stock market's growth, up to a cap. As of this writing, those caps tend to be around 11–12 percent. So, if the market goes up 10 percent next year, you would get 10 percent growth in your policy. If the market goes up 15 percent, you would get the cap of 11.5 percent, for example.

Here's the special magic: Your account has a floor of zero. This means the least amount of interest you can be credited in a year is zero percent. If the market drops 15 percent this year, your account receives no interest . . . but it doesn't lose any value, either. It just stays where it is.

In the following chart, the bottom line represents $100,000 invested in the S&P 500®, including dividends — the most common measure of the stock market, as you may remember. This is the same line we examined earlier in the book. As you can see, after the tech bubble burst in 2000, the market dropped for three straight years. It built back up through the middle of the decade and then dropped again when the real estate bubble burst. At the end of last year, after eighteen years in the market, your $100,000 grew to $246,507, for an average total return of 4.86 percent a year.

We've already discussed the problems you face when only earning an average of 4.8 percent on your savings and how, minus fees and taxes, that's just not enough growth for the retirement income you'll likely want in the future.

Now, let's do a comparison and see how indexing performed during this same period.

The top line of the chart represents the concept of indexing inside an IUL policy.[13] Look at the difference in growth. You can see that, by eliminating the down years of the market, your account never loses value and therefore can grow money much more efficiently.

---

[13] The indexed example utilizes a hypothetical index with a cap of 11.5% and a floor of zero percent. It does not reflect expenses or any specific product or policy.

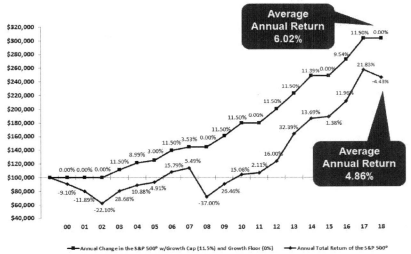

As you can see, when the market is crashing from 2000 to 2002, the IUL policy is credited zero percent. Those are some of the happiest years, because everything else is losing money while you're holding your own. In 2003, when the market turns around, the indexed policy begins net-positive growth immediately. It doesn't have to dig out of the hole from the market drop, because the index resets every year at the market's current level. Again, in 2008, the policy is credited zero percent, and the next year immediately beings net-positive growth again.

So, at the end of eighteen years, the $100,000 inside the index has grown to $303,845. That means the total amount of interest credited to your account averages 6.02 percent a year.

Let's look at an even scarier market: the "lost decade of investing" from 2000 to 2009. As you remember, it encompasses the market crashes of 2000 and 2008, as well as some of the market recovery.

During this decade, the S&P 500® (including dividends) returned an average of NEGATIVE 1 percent a year. No wonder 2000 to 2009 has earned the title of worst decade in the history of the S&P 500®.

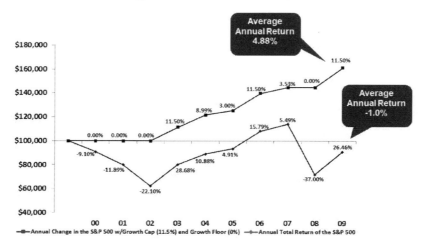

Indexing performed much better. By eliminating just a few bad (negative) years (2000 to 2002 and 2008), and instead making them zero percent credited interest, the index had an average annual credited rate of 4.88 percent. That's not too shabby in a market that is losing money!

Indexing lets you capture a good portion of the upside, with no downside risk. Once that interest is credited to your account, you never give it back, even if the market subsequently drops. As a result, it creates a return pattern that is incredibly powerful.

This is one valuable way you can eliminate compromises in your retirement savings. With indexing, it doesn't matter when you want to retire: When the market is strong, your account is growing. When the market is down, your account value stays protected. You don't have to earn back market losses, like with mutual funds in a

401(k) or IRA. Indexing delivers a steady, predictable growth pattern — just what you need in retirement.

What's the Worst That Can Happen?

By now, you've probably noticed I'm a big fan of indexing. It's an incredibly powerful way to grow funds when the market is up while also protecting them when the market is down.

But — as an actuary — I wasn't finished crunching numbers.

One afternoon, chatting with my brother-in-law, I asked him what he thought was the scariest economic period is U.S. history. He gave the answer most people my generation give: the Great Depression. He and I had heard from our parents about the wild market swings that took place throughout the 1930s, and how the stock market collapsed on itself, destroying the savings of many, many Americans. It was truly an unprecedented time.

So, I decided to see how the Great Depression would have turned out for someone in an IUL policy. How would this strategy fare in one of the most turbulent economies our country has ever known?

First, let's look at what the stock market did during the Great Depression and the ensuing recovery.

Today, the S&P 500®, that measurement we've discussed of the 500 largest stocks, is the standard-bearer for how we measure a market's strength or weakness. Of course, in 1929, analysts didn't measure the top 500 stocks. Thankfully, academics have gone back and calculated how the top 500 stocks in the market performed in the 1920s and 30s.

Here's how those stocks performed:

Historical Total Returns (Including Dividends) of 500 Largest Stocks[14]	
Year	Performance
1929	-8.3%
1930	-25.1%
1931	-43.8%
1932	-8.6%
1933	+50.0%
1934	-1.2%
1935	+46.7%
1936	+31.9%
1937	-35.3%
1938	+29.3%

So, what happened to someone who, in 1929, invested $100 in the stock market? Five years after the Great Depression started, his $100 has been reduced to $53, which was mostly dividends. He lost 47 percent of his money.

Miraculously, after eight years, he was back to a little above break-even. The market rallied, and in 1937 he finally had more money than he started with.

Then the market crashed again. At the end of 1938, he had $84.64 in his pocket. What a decade!

Put another way, $100 invested in the stock market at the beginning of 1929 was worth about $35 by 1932. Despite the recovery that followed, by the end of the decade in 1938, his $100 investment was worth about $85.

---

[14] Aswath Damodaran. Stern at New York University. "Data." http://www.stern.nyu.edu/~adamodar/New_Home_Page/data.html

So, what would an indexed insurance product have looked like during the Great Depression? First, some assumptions. Let's give this index a floor of zero percent and a ceiling of 11.5 percent. Secondly, we'll continue using those same back-projected estimates of the S&P 500®, since that measurement didn't exist in the 1930s.

Here's what indexing looked like in the Great Depression:

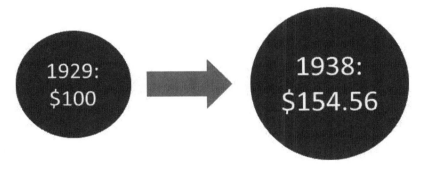

Pretty amazing, right? The $100 in our hypothetical index would be worth $154,56 by 1938. That's an average growth rate of 4.45 percent a year . . . during the GREAT DEPRESSION!

How is this possible? It all comes down to math. When you eliminate any negative years *and* you never give back the interest you've accumulated, it's easier to realize net-positive gains over the long run. During the Great Depression, everyone else was losing their wealth when the market dropped. But you, with your indexed account, just got zero percent interest that year. No big deal. The next year, you started growing again from a positive position.

This is why I love the concept of indexing.

But what do others say?

The Money Manager

I have a client named Will who is one of the smartest financial guys I know. Before he retired, he managed billions of dollars in institutional pension funds. Essentially, it was his job to grow enough money for a company to pay everyone their pensions.

Indexing piqued his interest. But, of course, he wanted to run his own analysis.

So, he back-tested indexing in numerous historical periods. How would it perform when the market was down, up or on a roller coaster ride? What about in times of slow growth? Fast growth?

When we sat down one January afternoon, he set a ream of paper on the table, heavy enough to make a thud. This was his analysis. I asked him what he had determined, and here's what he told me:

"Marty, the return pattern in this product is so unique, it's unlike anything else in my portfolio. I think everyone should own an asset like this."

Translation into non-money-manager speak? The balance of protection and growth is unlike anything else. Everyone needs to take advantage.

Pretty high praise from a guy who was used to working with the stock market.

Now you see why.

CHAPTER SEVEN

Eliminating the Conflict of Income vs. Legacy

Here's where many people stop and say, "Marty, I get it. Insurance has a death benefit. I can use it for my legacy."

And they're right. In fact, when most people think about life insurance, they don't think about indexing and account value accumulation. They think about protecting their family with a death benefit.

That's why IUL is able to eliminate the conflict of income vs. legacy in your IRA.

But there is so much more than that. IUL is a savings vehicle with a death benefit above and beyond the account value in the policy. More than that, the interplay of these two features creates an instrument that delivers value like nothing else I've seen. Let's dive in and I'll show you why.

The Four Big Needs in Retirement

If you remember back in Chapter Three, I outlined four big ways you may need to use your retirement funds:
1. As income for planned expenses
2. For unplanned emergency expenses

3. To cover the medical costs of aging
4. To leave as a legacy for your heirs

Let's take a look at how IUL performs when it comes to each of these scenarios.

Getting Your Money

First, let's talk income, the primary reason you've been saving for retirement all of these years.

IUL policies have a cash value, which is the account value of the policy. Remember last chapter, when we discussed indexing? The cash value is the funds that grow through indexing.

The cash value works similarly to other savings instruments you may be familiar with: When you pay premiums, the money goes into the cash value of the IUL policy. Then, expenses are deducted, and interest (through indexing) is applied.

In retirement, you can access funds from your account value as income.

This is where an IUL policy varies a little from your 401(k) or IRA. In an IRA, you withdraw $50,000 and get a check for $50,000 (which, less taxes, is your retirement income). Your IRA balance is lower by $50,000.

In an IUL policy, you borrow $50,000 through a policy loan. You still get a check for $50,000 (and those funds are tax-free, so you can spend all $50,000). But really what you are doing is borrowing against your death benefit.

When I say "loan," your first thought is probably, "Why would I want retirement income I have to pay back?" But that's not really how it works. Let's say you have a one million dollar death benefit, and over your lifetime your "loan" grows to $800,000. When you die, the one million dollars first goes to pay off the $800,000 loan.

The remaining $200,000 then goes to your heirs, tax-free, as a legacy.

I won't go much deeper into loans (I could write a whole book on those alone!), but it's enough to say that most IUL policies have an option to access your funds with minimal or no net interest charged.

The end result is the same: IUL policies deliver checks with income you can spend, just like pulling funds from your 401(k) or IRA. But with IUL, you won't owe any taxes on that check.

Your Money, Undiscounted

Now you know how you access funds from an IUL policy. But that's not the exciting part about loans.

I was reminded of the value of IUL loans by one of my clients, Daniel. Daniel had a brokerage account through his bank, and in 2009 he and his wife decided to buy a condo in Florida. He needed to use some of the funds in his brokerage account, but when he went to withdraw them, he was met with a dilemma: The market was down dramatically as the housing bubble burst. He could access his money, but it was discounted around seventy-five cents on the dollar. That means his account had lost about a quarter of its value, and any money he pulled out was now "costing" him more than it would have a year earlier.

Daniel began to understand the impact of market-value adjustment.

If you have a stock worth $60 a share today, you can sell it for $60. But if the value of that stock drops to $30, you now have two options: Wait for the value to grow to $60 again, or sell it at $30 for a 50 percent market value adjustment. If you need $60 from your stock account today, you'd have to sell two shares of stock rather than one.

This is what occurs every time you withdraw money from your IRA or 401(k): You withdraw funds at the current value of your account. For people like Daniel who need funds when the market is down, this means they have to discount the funds they can access. This is why, as we age, we tend to move our portfolios into more secure models; we can't risk the money not being there when we need it.

IUL policies don't share this problem.

Remember when we discussed indexing? Interest credits cannot be less than zero. So that means, even in 2008 when the market dropped, IUL policies didn't receive negative interest (i.e., lose money). They were just credited zero percent interest. The account didn't grow, but their funds weren't taken away by the market, either.

The zero percent floor means funds accessed from IUL policies never have a market-value adjustment. If you need $50,000, you can get that money from your full account value, not discounted rate.

That is a huge benefit of saving in IUL.

Help for the Medical Cost of Aging

Another thing that attracted me to IUL? It can deliver additional funds to cover long-term care needs.

Every IUL policy is different, but many IUL policies have additional funds that can be used for the medical costs of aging. These policies enable you to borrow from the higher death benefit amount for certain medical needs. The result? You can access more money than is in your account to cover the medical cost of aging.

Basically, it would be like walking into the bank and saying, "I have a $20,000 CD, but I have long-term care needs, so please give me $30,000 for it." The banker would look at you like you're crazy! What would happen if you went to your stockbroker and said, "I'm going into a nursing home, so please cash out my $20,000 brokerage account for $30,000." Your stockbroker would say, "The account is worth whatever it's worth. That's all I can give you for it."

But with IUL, because of the death benefit, you can access funds from a much higher amount than your account value.

If you ultimately decide IUL may be a beneficial approach for you and retirement health costs are a concern, be sure to find an advisor who understands IUL and can direct you to policies with good living benefits.

Legacy for Your Heirs

I started this chapter stating the obvious: IUL overcomes the conflict between income for you and legacy for your heirs.

That's because your policy delivers a death benefit above and beyond the account value.

If you have a $2 million IRA and you die, your heirs get $2 million, *less taxes*. That's because, whether you're living or dead, your IRA is just worth its account value, less taxes.

But IUL is different. In an IUL policy, your $2 million cash value might deliver a $2.5 million death benefit. So there are additional funds for your heirs — and they're delivered tax free.

Consider this: If you died today with a $2 million IRA, it might deliver $2 million less taxes to your heirs. At a 25 percent tax rate, let's call it around $1.5 million. But your IUL could deliver $2.5 million *tax-free*. Pretty easy choice, right?

IUL — and life insurance, more generally — is the only option that truly overcomes the conflict between what you spend while living and your ability to leave something to your heirs after you're gone.

And that's how IUL eliminates conflict No. 2.

CHAPTER EIGHT

Eliminating the Conflict of You vs. Uncle Sam

Here's our final conflict: You vs. the IRS. How much of your account is yours, and how much is Uncle Sam's?

Let's think back to the tax chapter. As you remember, there are three main kinds of savings approaches:

- **Taxable**, which means you pay taxes on the original income, and then continue to pay taxes on any gains you make from accumulated interest or growth.
- **Tax-deferred**, which means you do not pay taxes on your contributions today, but you pay taxes on your contributions and all the earnings in your account when you get the money in retirement. This is your typical 401(k) or IRA.
- **Tax-free**, which means you pay taxes now on your contributions, but then they grow tax-free. When you go to retire, you don't owe any taxes on the money when you receive it. This is how Roth IRAs work, and also how IUL works.

Properly structured, you can access funds from an IUL policy completely tax-free. That's what Section 7702 of the U.S. Tax Code allows. The funds you grow in your policy can be used with no tax due.

Remember the tax analysis I ran on my IRA?

RMD Analysis on Martin's Qualified Accounts (reinvested RMDs)	
Assuming a 25% tax liability, 5% pre-tax growth with equivalent reinvestment growth	
Receive RMDs to age 90	Per IRS rules
Total taxes paid on RMDs	$221,223
Taxes paid on growth of reinvested RMDs	$90,714
Taxes paid by heirs on remaining IRA value at death (age 90)	$142,587
TOTAL TAXES PAID	**$455,524**

I said it was like a highway with two exits. On one exit, if I convert to tax-free, I pay a $175,000 toll right now, and then can get to my destination without paying anything else. On the other exit, I stop at tollbooth after tollbooth until I've paid $455,524 to get to my destination.

IUL lets you get to your retirement destination without paying that tax at the tollbooth every year.

Kicking the IRS to the Curb

Remember when I said the IRS was a silent partner in your retirement account? Its partnership comes with a lot of rules, too.

When you save in a tax-deferred account, you're subject to a variety of rules around when you can access your funds. You're probably familiar with the two most common:

- **You cannot access funds from your IRA or 401(k) before age fifty-nine-and-one-half.** If you do, you'll pay an additional 10 percent tax penalty on the withdrawn funds. This is to make sure people are using the tax deferral for long-term savings, and not to quickly lower their tax bracket in a given year.

- **You MUST access a portion of your funds starting at age seventy-and-one-half.** This is the required minimum distribution we discussed. At age seventy-and-one-half, the government requires you to withdraw a certain amount of your qualified fund. Why? Because they want to tax it! Uncle Sam is saying, "You have deferred your taxes long enough. Now we want our revenue."

Do these rules apply to IUL?

No.

That's because you're not saving under Section 401(k). You're saving under Section 7702 — and the IRS doesn't have these tax penalties or RMDs under Section 7702.

This gives you more flexibility for your funds. You can access them when you need them, not when the IRS says you can.

Personally, I don't plan to retire at age seventy. I love my work, and I plan to keep working. There's a good chance I won't need to start taking money out of my IRA when I'm seventy — at least not out of some of my accounts. But in an IRA, the IRS says I have to take out money whether I need it or not. That means less money earning interest in my account and more money being taxed each year.

You can imagine how glad I am IUL doesn't have that restriction.

Brief and to the Point

This is a pretty short chapter. I know I don't have to sell you on the benefits of saving tax-free rather than tax-deferred. We took care of that in Chapter Four.

So I'll just say this: as an actuary, I'm trained in protecting against risk. And protecting against risk is all about protecting against the worst-case scenario. When saving for retirement, the worst case for taxes is paying more than you have to over your lifetime. IUL is a sterling way to eliminate tax risk from a portion of your retirement assets.

You have a rare, once-in-a-generation opportunity right now. Thanks to the tax overhaul passed by Congress in December 2017, many savers are in lower tax brackets now than they were before. That means they can convert portions of their retirement funds to tax-free strategies at lower rates than they could have just a few years ago.

Remember what I said? These lower tax rates won't last forever. They expire in 2025. So, the time to act is now.

If there's one commitment you make after reading this book, let it be this: make this year the year you quit compromising by giving Uncle Sam part of your retirement account.

I'll show you how in the next chapter.

CHAPTER NINE

Putting My Money Where My Mouth Is

If you remember back in the introduction to this book, I said this book was my story: it's the story of how I chose to do something different — something better — with my IRA.

To close this book, I want to share with you what I did to overcome the conflicts in my IRA.

Following is the strategy I took. I've shared this strategy with dozens of leading CPAs across the country, who have all responded with enthusiastic support. (In fact, several of the CPAs have chosen to use this approach with their own retirement funds, and many more have recommended it to their top clients.) In short, they all agree: it works.

So, here are the steps I took.

First, I completed my analysis. I looked at the total tax liability in my IRA (high), and what that tax liability would be in a tax-free vehicle (much lower). I considered my income and legacy needs (I'd like to have both). I reviewed how likely it was to both grow and protect my funds in today's market (not very).

After my analysis, I decided to take action.

Here's what I did.

A Different Kind of Conversion

You're probably familiar with the concept of Roth conversions. This strategy has gained increasing popularity over the past decade as more savers come to realize the Great American Savings Myth. It's fairly straightforward: if you have money in a tax-deferred account but would rather have those funds growing in a tax-free account, you can "convert" your tax-deferred funds into tax-free funds.

How? You withdraw funds from your qualified account, like your 401(k) or IRA. You pay taxes on the funds you've withdrawn, and you put the remaining amount into a Roth IRA or Roth 401(k) account, where they then grow tax-free.

While Roth conversions are by far the most common approach, they are not the only option for converting your funds into tax-free assets. You can also do an IRA-to-IUL conversion, which is rapidly growing in popularity for the reasons outlined in this book.

The concept is the same: you withdraw funds from your qualified account. You pay taxes on those funds, and you put the net funds in an IUL policy (usually over a few years, through premium payments).

From there, the funds grow tax-free in the IUL policy, can be accessed for tax-free income, and pass on to your heirs, tax-free.

That's the approach I took.

How Much to Convert?

As I mentioned, my goal was to diversify the tax status of my retirement accounts, getting more funds into tax-free vehicles. My wife and I have several retirement savings accounts, but the largest is my IRA. We looked at our retirement funds and decided how much to dedicate to this strategy.

As an actuary, I knew IUL policies delivered the most value if you give them around ten years to accumulate. Since I was sixty-six at the time, I set a goal of using my IUL funds around age seventy-six. Although I wanted to convert everything I had into a tax-free IUL, that wasn't a reasonable goal. I kept enough money in my current accounts to fund our retirement needs for the next few years.

At first, my wife wasn't thrilled I was recommending we wait ten years to use the funds in our IUL policy. But then I gave her a simple explanation and changed her mind.

Think about having two pots of money. In pot A, you earn a dollar and get to keep seventy-five cents. In pot B, you earn a dollar and get to keep a dollar. Which pot of money do you want to grow? The one where growth only gets you seventy-five cents on the dollar, or the one where growth nets you the full dollar?

Pot A is your IRA or 401(k). You want to spend that money first. After all, growing that money long-term is less advantageous to you, since you will owe taxes on that growth. Pot B is your tax-free IUL policy. Every dollar of growth in that policy is yours to keep. So, it makes sense to spend those funds later in retirement, since you're not penalized by the IRS for its growth.

My wife and I won't be delaying our retirement income with this strategy. Instead, we're just using our remaining IRA money in the near term and relying on our IUL funds later in retirement.

In the end, I decided to take $500,000 from my IRA and place it in an IUL policy. IUL would represent the tax-free portion of our money that would fund our later-years retirement.

Confidence in My Choice

When I told my brother-in-law about what I did, he pointed out a benefit I hadn't realized. One of the biggest risks with a Roth conversion is this: What if I withdraw my money, pay all those taxes, and die before I earned back the taxes I paid? After all, if I withdrew $500,000 from my IRA, I would only net about $375,000 after taxes to put in my Roth IRA.

With IUL, that's not a concern; I have a death benefit that would more than make my heirs whole if for some reason I die too soon.

Likewise, if I converted my IRA to a Roth all in one year, I would probably put myself in a higher tax bracket the year I converted the funds. But tax law requires premium payments for tax-free IUL to be spread out over several years; I'm withdrawing 20 percent of the account each year for the next five years. This spreads out the tax impact and lets me maintain my current tax bracket.

Sometimes, I refer to this strategy as a Roth conversion on steroids: Like a Roth conversion, I've converted my tax-deferred assets into tax-free funds. But, rather than putting my money in a Roth IRA, which has the same conflicts of growth vs. security and income vs. legacy, I've put my funds into a vehicle that eliminates those conflicts, too.

By now, you know I'm an actuary and numbers drive my decisions. So, here's what my wife and I have gained by using IUL for a portion of our retirement savings, according to my calculations:

- We're saving hundreds of thousands of dollars in taxes from our retirement funds.
- We're increasing the amount of after-tax income we can access in retirement.
- We're eliminating market volatility from impacting our savings.

Do those sound like three benefits you want in retirement, too? Now you know how to get them.

CHAPTER TEN

Too Good to be True?

At this point, you're probably thinking, "Hm. IUL can eliminate the major conflicts in my IRA. That's great, but..."
And you're not quite sure what the *but* is about.

Maybe it all sounds too good to be true?

I've talked about IUL as a retirement savings approach to hundreds of people like you. I get this question nearly every time: "This sounds great, but what's the catch?"

The truth is, there isn't much of a catch. Like any financial decision, it's important to work with a qualified professional, and it's important to make sure the strategy meets your personal goals and needs.

That's why I always encourage good due diligence from my clients. It's important to ask questions and feel like the answers put you at ease.

Here's the deal: you're smart. I know you're smart because people who aren't smart don't make it to Chapter Ten in a book about saving.

What do smart people do when they hear about an idea that's new to them? They Google it.

I would, too.

Of course, there are detractors from any financial strategy. So, let's talk about the top concerns you find when you Google "using IUL for retirement savings."

Truthful Scale

As an actuary, I believe in dispelling myth with fact. Following, I've outlined the most common objections to using IUL for retirement savings, and rated how truthful they are using the "Truthful Scale" below. One star means the objection is not truthful: the objection is likely based on misinformation or is intended to misinform. Two stars means the objection has some truth to it, or it may be true in some situations. Three stars means the objection is truthful and you should pay attention to it.

Truthful Scale:
* Not truthful. Likely based on misinformation or intended to misdirect.
** Somewhat truthful. May be true in some situations.
*** Truthful. Evaluate this objection carefully.

Objection: Structure

"IUL is pretty complex, and if it's structured wrong, you could get a raw deal."

Truthful Scale: ***

IUL can be structured many ways, and not all of those structures deliver the most value to you. Always work with a highly qualified professional on your IUL policy. I worked for a month to develop the perfect structure for my plan, and it's a structure we now use with most of our clients. IUL must be structured properly to deliver all the benefits we've discussed in this book. If you need help finding someone reputable in your area who uses a proven structure, call our office and we can help you identify the right professional.

Objection: Unrealistic Proposals

"They're making IUL look better than it is by using unrealistic assumptions about future growth."

Truthful Scale: **

It's impossible to predict what any financial instrument will do in the future. The best we can do is look at past performance and project that forward. It's true with IUL, and it's true with 401(k)s, IRAs and most financial products. However, IUL has the power of indexing. If you remember from our discussion of indexing, it helps stabilize the growth of your funds, because there are no negative years to deal with. While the market may be up 30 percent one year and down 40 percent the next, indexing is more stable and thus less susceptible to unrealistic assumptions than other financial products.

This is one of the reasons I always show my clients some "worst case" scenarios, and why in this book I wanted to show how indexing could perform in terrible markets, like the Great Depression and the "lost decade of investing."

To get a complete picture, talk to your advisor about the full range of potential results.

Finally, I'm glad that industry regulators have recently established new rules to help prevent any advisors from showing projections that are too aggressive or unreasonable.

Objection: Expense

"Never use insurance to save for retirement. It's so expensive!"

Truthful Scale: *

Here's one of my favorite myths about IUL, because it's so easy to dispel. There's a common refrain that life insurance is too expensive to use as a savings tool. What this means is that life insurance contains fees. So do 401(k)s. [15] And IRAs. [16] And Roth IRAs. [17] So, when people tell me, "IUL is too expensive," I always ask them, "Compared to what?"

Let's look at the fees you could pay in each kind of account.

401(k)	IRA	IUL
Administrative Fees Pay the company administering your account	Advisor Fees Pay the person managing your funds for managing your account	Mortality Fees Support your life insurance death benefit
Management Fees Pay for asset management in certain kinds of funds	Managed Account Fees Pay for the creation of a portfolio within your account	Expense Fees Support the expenses of establishing, underwriting and managing your account
Fund Fees Fees for the mutual funds or other funds in your account	Fund Fees Fees for the mutual funds or other funds in your account	

---

[15] U.S. Department of Labor. "A Look at 401(k) Plan Fees." http://www.dol.gov/ebsa/publications/401k_employee.html.

[16] Robert Powell. MarketWatch. Aug. 10, 2010. "No free lunches, no fee-free IRAs." http://www.marketwatch.com/story/no-free-lunches-no-fee-free-iras-2013-08-10.

[17] Society for Human Resource Management. Feb. 28, 2013. "401(k) Plan Fees Declined — Slightly — in 2012." http://www.shrm.org/hrdisciplines/benefits/articles/pages/401k-feeseclined.aspx.

As you can see in the preceding chart, there are a variety of fees in all products. Fees are how the companies providing these savings vehicles make money. Fees have to be an accepted part of your retirement savings plans.

But you don't want to pay more fees than necessary. The average cost for a 401(k) plan with fewer than one hundred employees is 1.4 percent. For a plan with more than one hundred employees, it's 1.03 percent.[18] That fee is charged on your funds every year as you're working and contributing money, and when you're retired and drawing down money.

If you are in a 401(k) plan, not only are you paying an administrator to manage the 401(k) plan itself, but every time you put money into a mutual fund you have an additional set of fees you're paying. What do those fees buy you? Well, you get access to mutual funds, and some investment advice.

In an IUL policy, you pay a cost of insurance fee and general expense fees. For these fees, you get some real benefits: a death benefit, tax-free savings growth and, of course, **the power of indexing** to grow your funds over time.

Sure, you're thinking, you get a lot for those fees. But the fees are still so high!

That's What Neil Thought

If you've read my first book, you may remember this story. I'm including it again because it's such a compelling one.

Neil, a team member in my office, came to us from the world of managed money. His background is in investing, and he didn't trust

---

[18] Robert Powell. MarketWatch. Aug. 10, 2010. "No free lunches, no fee-free IRAs." http://www.marketwatch.com/story/no-free-lunches-no-fee-free-iras-2013-08-10.

life insurance as a savings vehicle. Why, you might ask? He had always been told it was too expensive.

When he started working with us, he always came back to cost: "But how can we recommend something with such high fees?"

I wasn't convinced the fees were so high. Being an actuary, I decided to look at the numbers.

First, I wanted to compare apples to apples. In a managed account like an IRA or 401(k), fees tend to stay uniform as a percentage of assets throughout the life of the account. For example, this year you might owe 2 percent in fees on your account that currently has $100,000 in it. You would pay $2,000 in fees. You will likely owe that same 2 percent of fees in twenty years, when your account has grown to, say, $500,000. That year, you would owe $10,000 in fees. In an IUL policy, fees are structured differently. In these products, fees are typically front-loaded to pay a higher percentage on assets in early years, when the account balance is low. That means you're paying more fees when you have a little money, and dramatically less in fees when your account has grown. So, to compare fees in both products, I had to convert an IUL's fees into an annualized percentage, just like in a 401(k).

I took Neil, who was forty at the time, and compared the fees he was paying in his 401(k) to the fees he'd pay in an IUL policy. Then we pitted the average annual fee from both strategies against each other.

What we discovered blew Neil away, and made him a true believer. I think it will blow you away, too.

The advisors Neil had been working with in his previous job usually charged their clients around 1 percent for their services. When added to mutual fund fees and other fees, their clients were paying 2 percent or more in portfolios that boasted about their low-cost nature.

How did IUL fare? In one IUL product I examined, Neil would be paying, on average, 0.76 percent of his annual account value in fees.

For half the cost of the average 401(k) and a third of the cost of the average advisor-managed account, Neil could access all the benefits of IUL.

(I know you're curious: What was the cost of my IUL policy? After all, my wife and I are in our sixties. It has to be expensive, right? Well, in our plan, my wife and I expect our expenses to average around 1.22 percent a year — less than I pay in most of my retirement accounts.)

The bottom line? When IUL is properly structured to also help you save, the policies can have very competitive costs and deliver a lot more for those fees, too.

In short, don't ever let anyone tell you life insurance is too expensive a way to save.

Now you know better.

CHAPTER ELEVEN

Final Thoughts

I wrote this book to tell my story: How an actuary who had spent his life analyzing risks associated with saving had fallen victim to the Great American Savings Myth of tax-deferral . . . and found his way to something better.

I wrote it to stop people like you from falling for the Great American Savings Myth as well. To help you quit accepting compromise in your retirement accounts. To eliminate the conflicts in your IRAs and 401(k). Above all, I wrote it to help you realize the full benefit of the retirement funds you've saved.

But the book is ending, and you're probably thinking: what now? Well, that is up to you.

Fat-Free Frozen Yogurt

If you're a Seinfeld fan like me, you've undoubtedly taken more than a few life lessons from the TV show that's just supposed to make you laugh. But there's one episode that sticks out in my mind when I think about people mindlessly saving in their 401(k)s and IRAs.

Do you remember the Seinfeld episode where Kramer invests in a fat-free frozen yogurt shop? It's the hot new hit in town, and

George, Elaine, and Jerry find themselves eating there almost daily. After all, the frozen yogurt is so flavorful, so delicious . . . and it's fat-free! There's no guilt in eating it.

A few weeks later, Jerry and Elaine are perplexed. None of their clothes fit. They've put on seven or eight pounds. They can't figure out what happened.

Until they remember the fat-free frozen yogurt.

No, says Kramer. It can't be the yogurt. The yogurt is fat-free. It's good for you.

As we all know, it *was* the yogurt. Because fat-free doesn't mean calorie-free, nor does it mean sugar-free.

So why does this remind me of saving for retirement?

401(k)s and IRAs are the fat-free frozen yogurt of the savings industry. They have become the most popular way to save for retirement. People plow savings into them every day. And they feel good about it, because their money is growing tax-deferred. It's fat-free. It has benefits.

Of course, savers are overlooking the other features that matter when saving — the calories and sugar content, if you will. Is deferring your taxes helpful? What restrictions come with 401(k)s?

Much as it took weeks for Jerry and Elaine to discover the unsavory downside of yogurt (weight gain), most people don't realize the downside of their 401(k) or IRAs until later in life, when they retire and begin to understand the true repercussions of tax-deferred saving.

I want to steer you away from that fat-free frozen yogurt binge. Just because it's what you've been eating in the past doesn't mean you're helpless to change what happens in the future.

That's why I wrote this book.

What the Future Holds

Right now, whether you're forty, fifty, sixty, or seventy, you have a choice. With today's life expectancies, many Americans live nearly a third of their lives in retirement. That means you could have a third of your life to consider when choosing how to manage your finances going forward.

If you're like me, you've been dutifully saving in a 401(k) or IRA. And it can feel nerve-wracking to consider changing courses — especially this late in the game.

But a third of your life may be ahead of you! And NOW is the time for action.

I will end with this promise: if you evaluate your retirement account on the three compromises we've discussed — growth and security, income and legacy, your income and your taxes — you will approach retirement with a clear picture of where you are. And, if you believe as I do in the power of IUL we've discussed in this book, you can create a better plan to get where you want to be.

This is my story. I look forward to helping you write a happy ending to yours.

Addendum

Determine if IUL Might Be a Good Fit for You

One question I often hear after people read this book is this: "Okay. I believe in the power of IUL to overcome the conflicts in my IRA. But how do I know if this approach is right for *me?*"

First, let me say that, like many financial strategies, this approach can be beneficial for some savers, while not appropriate for others. Here are some guidelines to determining if this strategy might be right for you.

Finding the Right Help

There are many considerations you'll need to make when evaluating if a conversion strategy makes sense for you. That's why it's critical to find a financial advisor with expertise in two areas:

- Incorporating tax-efficient income strategies into retirement planning
- Using IUL as a tax-free vehicle for retirement funds

When evaluating your advisor or searching for a new one, make sure they fully understand the power of tax-free income and the unique features IUL can deliver. If you need help identifying an advisor who specializes in these areas, you can call my office and we'll work to connect you to a professional in your community.

Why is a good advisor so critical? As with any insurance strategy, proper structuring of the policy is critical to ensure your best interests are met.

As I mentioned, I've had teams of CPAs review this strategy, and all have told me the same thing: this absolutely works IF the strategy is structured properly. Following are the most important things for you and your advisor to consider.

How Can You Decide?

This is a two-step decision-making process:
- Does it make sense to save and grow a portion of your retirement funds in a tax-free vehicle, rather than the tax-deferred vehicle you're currently using?
- If the answer is yes, is IUL the *right* tax-free vehicle?

How Much Should You Allocate to This Strategy?

Most of the time, this strategy is not appropriate for your entire IRA account balance.

That's because funds in an IUL policy need time to accumulate. A good rule of thumb? Use this strategy for the portion of your IRA that is not needed for income in the next eight to ten years.

How Should My Advisor and I Evaluate My Current IRA/401(k)?

This book has outlined a sound alternative to qualified accounts. But it's impossible for a book to determine if that is the right approach for your individual needs. Here are the areas you and your financial advisor should evaluate:

- *Total tax liability*: How much in taxes will your 401(k) or IRA generate over your lifetime? Based on this analysis, you can decide if moving funds from a tax-deferred status to a tax-free status makes sense.
- *After-tax growth potential*: Using reasonable assumptions for growth and taxation, what would your after-tax IRA value be in ten, twenty, and thirty years?
- *Less favorable market growth*: What would happen to your IRA value if market performance is less favorable than assumed above?

How Can I Compare Results to an IUL Policy?

You should compare after-tax growth in your IRA/401(k) to after-tax growth in an IUL policy. Why after-tax growth and not just growth? After-tax growth is the money you actually get to keep. You should evaluate which strategy can provide more growth and income in terms of money you'll be able to spend.

Okay, now I'm going to get wonky. Feel free to stop here if you have enough information to make an informed decision. If you'd like to get into the weeds of how your funds will be converted from your IRA to an IUL policy, read on.

There are many nuances in a strategy like this. That's why it's critical to work with a financial advisor who understands both the IRA and IUL sides of this strategy.

If I Choose to Use IUL, How Should I Handle My Taxes?

You will owe taxes on the funds coming out of your IRA/401(k). After you withdraw your funds, you should set aside the portion representing the taxes, and put the remaining value into the IUL policy.

For example, if I withdrew $100,000 and had a 25 percent tax liability, I would set aside $25,000 for taxes, and put $75,000 into the IUL policy. (This math would be exactly the same if you were converting from your IRA to a Roth IRA.)

How Should My IUL Policy Be Structured?

Again, the most important thing you can do is work with an advisor educated in structuring IUL. You should rely on your advisor's recommendations, as he or she understands your personal situation and goals. However, here are some broad recommendations.

There are two key components to structuring an IUL policy appropriately:

- *How the policy is funded*: A five-pay premium pattern is generally the ideal structure for this strategy. That means you will be putting funds into your IUL policy over a five-year period. So, rather than withdrawing $100,000 from your IRA today, you would withdraw $20,000 each year for the next five years. Contracts that are five-pays work well to help maximize accumulation

while protecting the policy's tax-free status. In some cases, a seven-pay or even ten-pay may be appropriate to avoid moving you into a higher tax bracket in any given year.
- *How the death benefit is set*: The death benefit is an important consideration. After all, IUL can deliver something your IRA cannot: A legacy above and beyond the account value. In this strategy, it will often make sense to set the death benefit at the minimum allowed by IRS guidelines. Your advisor can help determine what this amount would be. This death benefit structure will protect the tax status of your funds, while allowing your account value to grow as quickly as possible.

Feel Good About Your Choice

You'll feel good about your choice if you're confident it's the right financial decision for you. Here's how you can do it:
- *Follow the results of your analysis.* Be sure to follow the results of the analysis above. In my experience, the analysis usually shows IUL to be the superior strategy — but not always. If you're in a situation where the analysis shows keeping your IRA to be the right decision, respect that analysis.
- *Evaluate cost.* Cost is one factor that can help establish why you may be better served by an IRA or IUL strategy. Look at the potential cost of both the IRA and the IUL policy over your lifetime.
- *Learn more.* The most important next step you can take? Find an advisor who specializes in tax-diversification, modern retirement strategies, and IUL. He or she can help you evaluate your current approach and, when

appropriate, design a better approach for your future. If your current advisor does not use these strategies as part of his or her practice, it may be time to find an advisor who does.

ACTING ON KNOWLEDGE

Pay It Forward

If you've read this book and been moved by its content, the first thing you should do is meet with a qualified financial advisor or insurance agent.

The second thing you should do? Pay it forward.

Pass this book on to a friend, relative, or colleague who would benefit from it. Help those you care about quit compromising in their retirement plans, too.

New Rules for the Next Generation

This book is all about eliminating compromises when you've saved in a tax-deferred account.

But what if you could help someone save the right way from the start?

Several places in this book, I referenced my first book, *The New Rules of Retirement Saving*. The book is aimed at professionals still in the active stages of saving — everyone from new college graduates and workers advancing in their careers to people beginning to think about retirement.

In the book, I share the story of how I helped my daughter, Rebecca, create a tax-free retirement for herself. Through her story, I discuss the three biggest risks today's savers face, and how proper planning can help overcome them.

If you have adult-aged children or grandchildren, or other professionals in your life who need to save the right way for their future, I highly recommend the book to them. I've included two chapters at the end of this book for your benefit.

Together, we can help the next generation save for retirement with the right rules, right strategies and right insights. If we help them now, they won't have to settle for compromises in the future.

~Martin H. Ruby, FSA

SELECTED EXCERPTS FROM

The New Rules of Retirement Saving

THE RISKS NO ONE IS TELLING YOU ABOUT . . .
AND HOW TO FIX THEM

Martin H. Ruby

STONEWOOD FINANCIAL
LOUISVILLE, KENTUCKY

CHAPTER ONE

The New Rules of Retirement Saving

"Invest in the future because that is where you are going to spend the rest of your life." ~ Habeeb Akande

I did it wrong.

That's not easy for a person like me to admit. I'm an actuary. And actuaries are mathematical experts at managing risk.

Yet I was blind to some of the biggest financial risks I'd ever face.

There's a good chance you're doing it wrong, too. This book is an attempt to fix that.

What is the "it" I'm referencing?

Saving for your future.

I know. Not the sexiest topic (except to actuaries like me). But it may be the most important thing you change this year.

So, what did I do wrong? I saved for the future in the wrong way.

It wasn't my fault. Not completely, anyway. I had a lot of people — experts among them — encouraging me to save this way. Now, at age sixty-five, I can see the tremendous mistakes I made.

Here's how I got into this predicament.

I graduated from Purdue University in 1972 with a degree in mathematics and physics. I was so eager to start my first job that I skipped my graduation ceremony altogether. While my classmates were tossing their hats in the air, I was settling into a new role as an actuarial student at Traveler's Insurance in Hartford, Connecticut.

At that point, saving for retirement was easy: I didn't have to do it personally because my company did it for me. In the 1970s, Travelers had a defined-benefit pension plan, so each year I accrued a portion of my salary that would be paid to me at retirement for the rest of my life. Amazingly, I didn't have to contribute a cent to this plan. It was up to my employer to fully fund it.

If only it had stayed that easy.

By the 1990s, I was CEO of an insurance company called Integrity Life, headquartered in Louisville, Kentucky. Here's where my savings plans went astray.

At Integrity, we didn't have a formal pension program. Instead, we saved in what was, at the time, the hot new savings product in America: the 401(k).

If you're reading this book, chances are you're saving in a 401(k), too. Chances are, if you don't make a change today, you're going to be facing the same risks I am in the future.

It doesn't have to be that way.

Here's the secret most financial experts know but aren't telling you: Today's most popular ways of saving for the future are creating some of the biggest risks in modern financial history. Yes, that includes 401(k)s and Individual Retirement Accounts, or IRAs.

What does that mean? This book will show you.

This book will teach you the New Rules of Retirement Saving and how you can use these rules to transform your savings strategy, eliminate risk, and increase your ability to enjoy the relaxing retirement you envision for yourself many years from now.

As you read this book, you may get a sinking feeling as you realize you've been saving for retirement in the wrong way. I'm here to tell you, it's not your fault. Our nation's savings infrastructure is slow to react when new risks develop, and most Americans are still saving under the old rules.

But you are responsible for what you do next. Don't save with the strategies of yesterday, strategies that can't overcome the risks of today.

Use these new rules of saving.

When you finish this book, I promise you'll feel more confident, more hopeful, and more prepared about your future and how to save for it.

I promise, if you follow the New Rules of Retirement Saving, you'll never have to start a book by writing, "I did it wrong."

Crisis in America

There's a crisis going on in America today, and you've inadvertently become part of it.

As a country, we have a problem using old financial strategies that no longer work to manage today's financial realities. We are using old rules to address new problems.

In most areas of life, we've kept up with the times. Certainly no one takes a photo at the beach with a Kodak camera, drives to the store, drops off the film, waits five days, and then picks up the prints. Today, you just snap a picture of that sunset on your phone and share it with the world via Instagram. Likewise, if you want to watch a movie on Friday night, you're more likely to order it on demand or via Netflix than to drive to a video store, pick out a DVD (or VHS!), and bring it home.

In fact, we're using new rules for most things we do. Do you bank online? Avoid eating too much red meat? Drive a car with an airbag? Research TVs online before buying one? In all these cases we've found better, more efficient, more rewarding ways to do many of the things we depend on for a happy life.

But not when we save for retirement. There, the vast majority of us still play by very old rules.

Your retirement savings represent your ability to enjoy a rewarding, happy future. Yet, most of us are using rules that are outdated, and worse, no longer valuable.

Imagine if every time you wanted to take a trip, you had to call the airline and have them mail you a ticket. That's the way it used to work. It's silly to accept that kind of inefficiency today, when you can get tickets electronically in a matter of minutes.

Or imagine if you broke your arm but didn't use an X-ray to see what's broken. For years, doctors had to guess what kind of fracture you had. Today, no one with access to good medical care would rely on guesses rather than X-rays.

When it comes to saving for retirement, most of us are making do with approaches that are as inefficient as mailing airline tickets and as risky as setting broken bones without X-rays.

It's time to update our rules.

They're All Talking About You

Do you know what they're saying about you? No, not your best friends or work buddies. I'm talking about the media. Fox News. Forbes. The New York Times. USA Today.

It's hard to find a news outlet these days that hasn't weighed in on the "savings crisis" in America. Most workers aren't saving enough for retirement — you may even be among them. That means you may be underprepared when your future arrives. Simply put, your retirement could be at risk.

And the media is right . . . to a point.

What the media is missing is that it's not your fault. You and your friends undoubtedly care about your future. You're saving. You're just saving under an old set of rules!

Because you're saving under an old set of rules, saving has become so problematic, so unrewarding, that many of your peers have given up all together. The rest of you do it out of obligation, but not with any measurable satisfaction.

This book is a guide to breaking that cycle.

Yes, I'm Talking to YOU

Are you saving in a 401(k) or IRA? Great job! You're doing more than many Americans.

I know it's tempting to say, "This book isn't for me. I already know what I'm doing."

But this book is for you. It's for every saver who has been misled by what's popular in today's savings market, with little regard for whether what's popular is also what's successful.

So, before we begin, let me say: I *am* talking to you. I promise. If you're like the vast majority of savers today, no matter how smart you are, you're saving under the old rules.

The Old Rules of Retirement Saving

Save through your employer. Invest in the market. Defer your taxes.

Lots of today's common savings rules were created for a far different kind of saver.

They were created for savers like my Uncle Irwin. Irwin would be eighty-eight this year, and he did something that is pretty foreign to most people reading this book: He worked for the same company his entire career. Irwin worked his way up the ranks, from salesman to management and finally to the senior leadership team. As a reward for his decades of loyalty, when Irwin retired, his company gave him a pension. During his later working years, he also saved in a 401(k), which his company matched handsomely.

The current rules of saving were created for people like Irwin. They were created for a time when employers shouldered most of the financial commitment for an employee's retirement fund, either through pensions or high 401(k) matches. My uncle didn't contribute much to his retirement accounts: his pension was entirely funded by his company, and his 401(k) was heavily subsidized by his employer. Most of his annual salary went to daily use, not long-term savings.

If you're reading this book and you have a pension like Irwin, good for you! Keep on saving under the old rules.

If you're reading this book and your employer matches 10 percent or more of your 401(k) contributions like my uncle's did, that's great! Keep saving under the old rules, too.

If you're like most Americans and you're saving for retirement without generous support from your employer, these rules aren't going to work for you.

That's why I've created a new set of rules.

Three Rules for a Better Future

This book is about the New Rules of Retirement Saving. It's about taking the same kind of insights and advancements that have taken place throughout our world and applying them to retirement saving.

These three rules are based on a blunt assessment of the risks you face today as a saver. Follow them, and you'll be on a better path to saving.

Why three rules? I could have created twenty or thirty new rules, from broad statements on savings philosophy to minutiae about daily savings activities, but I know you're not going to remember twenty rules. Besides, I've found it really boils down to three big actions. If you take these three actions, you'll be better prepared for retirement . . . not based on the past but based on the present and the future.

So, what are the three New Rules of Retirement Saving?

Rule No. 1: Know Your Risks
Rule No. 2: Choose a Strategy That Addresses Your Risks
Rule No. 3: Take Action Now

Sound simple? It's actually a fundamental shift from the way you're saving today.

Over the rest of this book, I'll help you learn about each rule and put it to work in your own savings strategy. By the end, you'll see how these three simple rules can transform your approach to the future.

CHAPTER TWO

Rule #1: Know Your Risks

"Risk comes from not knowing what you're doing." ~ *Warren Buffett*

Let's talk risks. You take risks into account more often than you probably give yourself credit for. Do you wear a seat belt? If you do, you are helping mitigate the risk of a fatal car crash. Do you eat fresh fruits and vegetables? With those wise dietary choices, you are helping address the risk of heart disease and other illnesses. Do you check the weather report before you leave the house? That is also a good idea. You're trying to eliminate the risk of getting drenched on your way to lunch.

Those risks are relatively easy to address because it doesn't take much to avoid them (I can buckle up in less than four seconds). Savings risk is different. It takes time to understand, and it takes commitment to change the way you're saving.

Your Three Biggest Risks

A book is sometimes an impersonal medium. When I meet with a client, I get to look at her across the table, get to know his family, or understand their financial situation. So, you might be thinking, "How can he know MY biggest risks?"

Here's a secret: Almost everyone is struggling with the same three risks. Read the following descriptions and think about whether they apply to you:

No. 1: Structural Risk — This risk is about the mechanics of saving. How are you saving? What savings vehicles are available to you? Who is helping you save? Is your employer contributing to your savings program? If so, how? Are government resources available to you? If so, what are they? Do you know which ones you should take advantage of and how to do so? How is your savings program structured? These questions can make the difference between whether you are successful or not, especially if your goal is to provide a comfortable retirement for yourself.

No. 2: Market Risk — Anyone who has followed the stock market over the last two decades is well aware of this risk. When you are saving money for your future, you want it to grow. Placing money in the stock market for that purpose comes with a risk that can best be illustrated by a pair of scales. Losses on one side. Gains on the other. The market giveth, and the market taketh away. This risk pertains to more than just Wall Street. Any time your savings are invested where loss is possible, whether it be stocks, bonds, real estate or a host of other assets, you face real risk that your savings will not experience sufficient growth to offset losses.

No. 3: Tax Risk — This risk is quite simple: How much of your retirement account will you get to use, and how much will you give to Uncle Sam in paying taxes? Tax risk is perhaps one of the most underappreciated risks today's savers face, and many Americans are doing nothing to address it. Many seemed resigned to pay any and all taxes presented to them as if there were absolutely nothing they could do about it. They believe Benjamin Franklin, who noted, "In this world nothing can be said to be certain but death and taxes." Or perhaps Will Rogers, who said, "The only difference between death and taxes is that death doesn't get worse every time Congress meets." "The uninformed taxpayer will pay much more in taxes than the informed taxpayer." I said that last one.

More than any other factors, these risks will impact how you save, how your money grows, and eventually, how you spend your money.

Encountering these risks one at a time is challenging enough, but you have to face all three, right now.

In the next chapters, we'll look at these risks one by one and help you assess how each risk may be impacting your retirement plans.

To read more from The New Rules of Retirement Saving, *find it as a Kindle download or paperback on Amazon at http://amzn.to/2FDmh4A*

ABOUT THE AUTHOR

Martin H. Ruby is a native of Louisville, Kentucky, where he lives and works. An actuary by profession, Martin serves as founder and CEO of Stonewood Financial. The company delivers actuarial expertise to clients building and managing wealth. In addition to serving his clients, Martin serves as a mentor for financial advisors adding tax-efficient planning to their practices, and he speaks nationally about the importance of tax-free income for today's retirees.

Before starting his own firm, Martin was CEO of a multi-billion-dollar insurance and annuity company, Integrity Life, where he led the growth of a successful retail annuity business, cutting-edge technology platforms, and innovative product development. He also served as head of the Life and Annuity Industry Group for Channel Point Technology and in several senior executive positions for Capital Holding Corporation (now part of AEGON).

Martin is a Fellow of the Society of Actuaries (FSA). He holds a Master of Business Administration degree from Bellarmine University and a Bachelor of Science degree in mathematics from Purdue University.

A dedicated community member, Martin has chaired and served on numerous boards for nonprofit and for-profit organizations, including Louisville Metro United Way, Jewish Hospital, and the Louisville Jewish Community Center. He is an active Angel Investor for start-up companies and enjoys mentoring emerging entrepreneurs.

Martin is married to his wife, Michele, who he met in first grade. They grew up together through junior high school and were in the same graduating class at Seneca High School in 1968. They married in 1971 and have two adult daughters, Becky and Sara. Both daughters are married to men both named Michael, and Martin and Michele have been blessed with four grandchildren: Robert, Molly, Andrew and George.

Martin gained an interest in the savings industry through his parents, Bob and Tess Ruby. Both were children of the Great Depression who instilled a strong work ethic and saving habit in their children. Bob and Tess put an emphasis on preparing for the future and valuing time spent with family. Martin works to accomplish these two goals every day in his life, as well.

ACKNOWLEDGMENTS

I am humbled to share my insights and passions with savers across the country. It's my greatest hope that I've helped you choose a better path to a happier retirement — one with fewer compromises and more value for you. But I didn't accomplish this alone. I want to thank several people who helped make this book possible. First, my daughter, Becky, who helped take my ideas and experiences and transform them into the moving book you're holding today. I'd like to thank my wife, Michele, a writer who helped make sure this book spoke to people with a wide range of financial knowledge. I'd like to thank the financial advisors across the country who are helping their clients stop compromising in their retirement accounts; their work is making a difference in the lives of millions of Americans. And finally, I'd like to thank my friends, colleagues, and clients who complained about their IRAs and the compromises they had to make. Their concerns became this book.

Made in the USA
San Bernardino, CA
17 June 2019